EXPANSIVE LOVE

of related interest

The Anxious Person's Guide to Non-Monogamy
Your Guide to Open Relationships, Polyamory and Letting Go

Lola Phoenix
Foreword by Kathy G. Slaughter, LCSW
ISBN 978 1 83997 213 3
eISBN 978 1 83997 214 0

How to Understand Your Relationships
A Practical Guide

Alex Iantaffi and Meg-John Barker
Illustrated by Jules Scheele
Foreword by Sophie Gamwell
ISBN 978 1 78775 654 0
eISBN 978 1 78775 655 7

Queer Sex
A Trans and Non-Binary Guide to Intimacy, Pleasure and Relationships

Juno Roche
ISBN 978 1 78592 406 4
eISBN 978 1 78450 770 1

Monogamy? In This Economy?
Finances, Childrearing, and Other Practical Concerns of Polyamory

Laura Boyle
ISBN 978 1 80501 118 7
eISBN 978 1 80501 119 4

EXPANSIVE LOVE

A Practical Guide to Relationship Anarchy

TUCK MALLOY

Jessica Kingsley Publishers
London and Philadelphia

First published in Great Britain in 2025 by Jessica Kingsley Publishers
An imprint of John Murray Press

2

Copyright © Tuck Malloy 2025

The right of Tuck Malloy to be identified as the Author of the Work has been asserted by them in accordance with the Copyright, Designs and Patents Act 1988.

Figure 4.1 recreated with the permission of Dr. Liz Powell; drlizpowell.com

This book contains mention of racism, homophobia, and transphobia.

A CIP catalogue record for this title is available from the
British Library and the Library of Congress

ISBN 978 1 80501 131 6
eISBN 978 1 80501 130 9

Printed and bound in Great Britain by Clays Ltd

Jessica Kingsley Publishers
Carmelite House
50 Victoria Embankment
London EC4Y 0DZ

www.jkp.com

John Murray Press
Part of Hodder & Stoughton Limited
An Hachette UK Company

The authorised representative in the EEA is Hachette Ireland,
8 Castlecourt Centre, Dublin 15, D15 XTP3, Ireland (email: info@hbgi.ie)

Contents

Introduction

Welcome to your practical guide to relationship anarchy. I'm very excited to be sitting here writing to you. I have dreamt of reading a book like this for quite a while. There have been insightful articles, quite a few clever zines, and a few books written on this topic, but I've found myself hungry for more. I feel lucky to contribute to the body of work and I am excited to welcome you into this contribution as well. As you read, digest, and share your experiences of this book you will birth more iterations, perspectives, and lived experiences of relationship anarchy. I am so excited to see what you all create, so thank you for being on this journey with me. How incredible it is that we are able to reach each other through time and space with words.

I have been practicing some form of relationship anarchy for most of my life, although much of that time I didn't name it as such. I was introduced to this term by a close friend when I was an undergrad at Reed College in Portland. As much as it helped me clarify my desires and approach to relationships, I have felt continually confused about what exactly relationship anarchy is, within myself and in my community. I wrote this book to explore the practical elements of relationship anarchy and elucidate how we can be in relationship with each other in a way that is ethical, ever-changing, and alive. My core question is, how do we build relationships that are loving? It may seem like a simple place to start, but I've found endless tributaries and rabbit holes to explore from this question. Loving other humans has always been at the center of my life, and for me, it's the one thing I care most about doing well. This includes loving others enough to protest the government when their rights are denied, loving others enough to understand how and why I hurt someone, and loving others enough to stay present in the pleasure of witnessing them grow.

For this reason, I knew writing this book would have to involve loving real humans in my world. This is how I decided to interview anyone who would talk to me about their experience of relationship anarchy. I have found that listening to another human with attentiveness and care is an intentional act of love, one that I choose over and over again whenever someone offers to share a piece of their heart with me. The heart of this book lies in these interviews. It became clear to me early on that the reason I am a relationship anarchist is the same reason I needed insight and help from others in order to write this book: My world makes sense because of other humans. Despite being an introvert and quite hermit-y (I love to stay home), there is nothing more important to me in this world than my relationships with other beings. My relationships with humans are the essential facilitator and framework for my connection with everything else.

To write this book I read every book, article, zine, Instagram post, and blog post on relationship anarchy I could find, and I spent many hours lying on my bed reflecting on my own experiences with relationship anarchy, trying to tease out what has made some of my relationships thrive and how others have led to heartbreak, grief, and loss. I spoke to countless relationship anarchists, polyamorists, thera-pists, coaches, activists, shadow workers, friends, partners, and monogamous people. Among these people, I specifically interviewed thirty humans who consented to sharing their lived experience with relationship anarchy. When choosing folks to interview, I prioritized humans who had the most intersections of marginalized identities, such as Black, Brown, Indigenous, disabled, queer, trans, fat, poor, immigrant, and/or sex workers. I gave my interviewees the option of being compensated for the time they spent being interviewed and/or receiving a free copy of this book, as well as having their business information included in the Resources section. I tried my best to let the voices of people I interviewed speak without much editing. I also encouraged my interviewees to edit and give feedback on the sections in which they are quoted. Each person is introduced with the identifying language that they requested, but these identifiers don't always encompass the diverse and nuanced reality of their lived experiences. If you want to learn more about the people interviewed here, you can find many of them in the Resources section of this book. I hope you seek them out because they are some of the greatest teachers I have had this past year. I was so consistently blown away by their insights, and I know y'all will be too.

Without humans I would not be able to commune with the trees the way I do, attune to my dog Amaro, or marvel at caterpillars inching along the leaves outside my window. My human attachments have defined my life in all ways, obvious and invisible. It seems completely fitting that I would end up writing a book about human relationships as I have often said to my friends and lovers that my number one goal in life is to love them and myself as fiercely and authentically as I can. This book has been a product of that fierce love. I have found—in exploring myself, the people I interviewed, and the connections I've formed over the years—that relationship anarchy feels more like an art form than a relationship style. This book contains many months of meeting other people, attuning to them, being with myself, processing rejection, celebrating connection, experiencing pleasure, pain, suffering, confusion, and all the spectrums of human emotion. There is a lot of me in this book because I didn't want to write a book that didn't have my heart in it. I hope as you read you will also bring yourself and your world into these stories, because this project of love really isn't possible without you.

I hope from this book you find a pathway into yourself and others. I invite you to begin this journey with writing a little bit about who you are. You can imagine you are introducing yourself to me. How did you end up here? Who are you? Which terms, words, and identities might you use to describe yourself? What does it feel like to be you?

If you're not sure how to approach these questions, I'd like to model for you what I mean. Let me introduce myself and this book to you. As you read about me and this project, I invite you to notice where you identify kinship and where you feel our differences. Which parts of this book do you yearn for, and which parts make you suspicious? What do you expect to experience here? What might this journey facilitate? All of it is welcome.

My name is Tucker Jade Malloy. I chose my own name with intention and love. I am white, queer, trans-masculine, non-binary, polyamorous, and a relationship anarchist. I'm also a sex educator and relationship coach. That's a lot of labels, so let me guide you in an exploration of how and why I wrote this book the way I did.

I am queer, which means to me that I fall in love with,

have sex with, and build relationships with all kinds of people, regardless of their gender. I also mean queer in the way bell hooks describes: "not who you're having sex with, but about being at odds with everything around it" (hooks 2014). My queer identity is much more than just who I am attracted to. It is a political, emotional, and relational orientation. I believe in celebrating non-normative, creative, and nuanced human experiences. My sexuality, gender, relationships, and experience of the world are inherently queer. I think of *queer* as a constant state of change and transformation. I seek to queer every space I set foot in, challenge the status quo, and destabilize norms whenever they stop serving human beings. From mycelium to stardust, I believe the universe is inherently queer.

I am also non-binary and trans-masculine, which means that I have transformed my body and self-presentation to align with what brings me the most joy, congruence, and inner peace. When I was born the doctors and adults around me decided that I should be raised as a girl because of the shape of my genitals. For the first twenty years of my life, I experienced a deep incongruence in my body and mind that was baffling and unsettling to me. As a teenager I would wonder, *Why do I hate being myself so much? Why do I love feminine people so much, but hate how everything feminine looks on me?* Unfolding answers to these questions came into focus for me when I began exploring my gender. As I supported the parts of myself that wanted to express and explore masculinity, I began to feel better and better. It's hard to describe how insatiably delight-ful it is to like yourself when you didn't before. I sought for something that would explain why I felt so miserable, and then I figured it out: I am a trans-masculine and non-binary human with a flexible and personal gender that I express through my clothes, body, affect, voice, and energy in different ways every day. I love the complex ways I feel and express my gender, which is why I identify as non-binary. As my eight-year-old buddy said to me recently, "I am not a girl girl or a boy boy or a really cool girl or a really cool boy or a boy or a girl or a boy and a girl I'm just kind of myself." So true, I said!

When I say I am a sex educator and relationship coach what I mean is that I spend most of my time teaching classes on sex and relationships and holding space for individuals and couples to explore their relationships, gender, sexuality, desire, and all the feelings that come with those journeys. I meet with quite a few couples and individuals weekly, while other folks reach out to me when they're having a particular struggle in non-monogamy, gender, sexuality, dating, relationships in general, or simply having a hard time in life. In 2020 I received a certificate as a holistic sex educator from the Institute of Sexuality Education and Enlightenment. In 2021, I started my business, IntraSensual Education, a sex education and coaching space that offers pathways to explore our bodies, senses, emotions, and life experiences.

When I say that I am polyamorous and a relationship anarchist, what I mean is that I love many people, and my relationships matter to me for lots of different reasons, in lots of different ways. I have multiple partners, friends, lovers, soulmates, and family members. My relationships grow organically, from the desires and capacities of the people I love. I use direct communication and consent to determine what kinds of activities the people I connect with want to share with me. I don't assume that someone who comes into my life will inhabit any specific role: I ask people what they want to do together, and if it's mutually agreed upon, we do the things. Sometimes my relationships make sense to other people and sometimes they don't. I will explain this in detail throughout this book, so don't worry if it's confusing right now.

I am a white European American living on unceded Ohlone land,[1] sometimes called the Bay Area. I have learned and I continue to learn from Black, Brown, and Indigenous people that whiteness is violent because of the way white supremacy has created systems of oppression that are perpetuated and upheld through "white body supremacy."[2] My whiteness is harmful in the ways it offers me comfort, stability, power, privilege, and status. And my light skin is not an inherently positive or negative part of my identity. I grew up in a white middle-class American family with generational wealth on both sides. My family is formed from both Protestant and Catholic traditions. Many of my ancestors are Irish people who resisted English colonialism, valued music and poetry, and joined in the creation of tight-knit, energetic families. There are also strong threads of white exceptionalism and elitism in my family culture, as well as patterns of abuse, neglect, alcoholism, and multi-generational trauma.

I am writing this book from the perspective that white supremacy is a violent system, one that we are all tasked with dismantling. Relationship anarchy is in alignment with this dismantling of systems, as it centers equity, collaboration, accountability, justice, and reconciliation. While I want to reduce the amount of harm I cause and I want to be a part of a pro-Black, pro-Brown, and pro-Indigenous revolution, I acknowledge that I am inherently limited by my whiteness in my ability to see and do what needs to be done. This is an

---

1   To learn about the land you occupy, check out https://native-land.ca/

2   In the book *My Grandmother's Hands*, Resmaa Menakem uses the term "white body supremacy" to describe the way white supremacy is enacted and perpetuated from the bodies of white people.

acknowledgment that everything I am doing is actively and intentionally in progress. The fact that I am writing about a relationship style that has ostensibly been appropriated from Indigenous cultures and re-labeled in a western context as "relationship anarchy" is problematic itself. My hope is not to bury or ignore the problematic aspects of my identity, my writing, my thoughts, and this work, but to elucidate why and how these things are problematic. And further, to explore how we might choose to continue to be in community with problematic, traumatizing, painful, harmful, and hurtful realities. Not to excuse or allow this suffering, but to acknowledge and tend to it.

It has been my experience that ignoring power differentials between myself and the people I love is much more harmful than identifying and being with the ways we continually miss each other. I hope through this book and through the community this book might create we can work together to deconstruct harmful power dynamics and replace these dynamics with relationships that feel truly supportive, equitable, and sustainable beyond the structures of white supremacy.

In this book, I center the stories and perspectives of the people who are living in non-normative relationships. The thoughts of Indigenous and/or Black and Brown people who I spoke to have been given intentional time, space, and attention in this book. That being said, I take full responsibility for the ways this book misses, harms, or invalidates certain experiences. My goal is not to avoid harm, because that would require never writing this book at all (or perhaps even never leaving my house again), but I do invite your experience to be exactly what it is. I invite your anger, your rage, your grief. I invite your euphoria, your joy, your pleasure. I invite your numbness, your neutrality, your uncertainty. I don't seek to change your experience of this book, but I do seek to offer some experience of change. Whether you leave this book further determined to never try something like relationship anarchy in your life—or decide to completely transform your relational landscape, or somewhere in between, or somewhere completely different than I can predict—I hope this book leaves you with something to think about.

The stories I heard from the people I interviewed changed me in profound ways. One of my first interviews was with Mora (they/them), a self-described "comrade, with a decent amount of experience in polyamory, solo, and relationship anarchy." They wisely shared that "the chaos of life takes smacks at you." After our interview I was reflecting on this comment, and I felt a wave of relief run from my head to my toes because I hadn't realized how intensely I had been trying to avoid being smacked at by life. Mora's charming humor and directness breathed such calm into my body; a reminder that I am not steering this ship, I am riding these waves. My hope is that you leave this book with some collected wisdom from those I've spoken to, and a deeper awareness of how humans may choose to relate to each other.

I often find that reading a book is a strange, disembodied experience of intimacy. I am a person who wrote these words in a particular moment of my life with a particular world around me. And you are a person reading these words (or listening) at a particular moment in your life with a particular world around you. We are connected, in a discourse, in relationship, and yet we may never discuss our thoughts face to face! I make a concerted effort to invite you into this book with questions, activities, and prompts. I also invite you to reach out to me during or after reading this book with feedback or comments. You can email expansivelove@gmail.com to share your experience.

I hope you give yourself whatever time and space you need to process this information, including taking breaks, reading out loud to yourself or listening to someone else, as well as putting this book down for months on end before you read it again. Feel free to start at the end and read backwards or open to a random chapter and go from there. This book is meant to be a tool, so I hope you write your thoughts down (in the margins or elsewhere) and read the quotes of people I've interviewed out loud so you can hear their voices more clearly. When you finish reading this book, I hope you think of how you could have written it better, and then I hope you do. I invite you to make this book into something you can use beyond the moments you read it. Whether that means giving it away to someone else or tearing out the pages for a collage, this book doesn't need to sit on your shelf gathering dust for years to come. If just one of you leaves this book with the idea of something to create, I will feel satisfied. That creation could be a relationship, a book or zine of your own, or a piece of art that illustrates your emotions. I can't wait to see all the things you create, and I hope you tell me about what you make; this project is just a drop of water in a river of thoughts, ideas, and creations that humans will bring into this world.

I think of this book as a love letter to my younger self. As I write these words, I am imagining all my younger selves playing together in the long, under-the-eaves closet of my childhood bedroom. Stuffed animals, dolls, books, and Legos are scattered on the floor. I imagine a teenage self sitting with my baby selves around them, reading this book out loud. Most of my inner children are calm and curious as they listen to these words. Some of them are skeptical, frightened, or shy. I wish I could go back in time and offer this wisdom, insight, and knowledge to an awkward and terrified 13-year-old Tuck as they embarked on the complexities of young love and friendship. I wonder if my younger selves could have been spared suffering or been held through their suffering if they had known about the many ways love can blossom. As much as I wish my inner children could read these words, I wish even more that the adults around me had had the knowledge and insight I have today. I love the saying, "you are the adult today that your younger self needed." And it's true; here we are.

Do you experience any of your inner children as I speak of mine? What would you want to tell a younger you about relationships if you could go back in time? How do you think a younger you would respond to meeting your current self? If you find it interesting to do, you can always write your own letter to your younger selves about the kind of love you dream of and what you've learned is possible. If you feel called, you can let your younger selves respond to your current self in letter form as well. Try writing with your non-dominant hand to invite an inner child to write you back.

The first chapter of this book will guide us through some of the historical and theoretical frameworks we need in order to understand how relationship anarchy came to be. We will explore how relationship anarchy is connected to white supremacy and to liberation of all humans. We will look at anti-colonial love and movements that transform the status quo. We'll unpack the ways marriage, romantic relationships, and gender norms have been utilized as tools of white supremacy to control and oppress people, but we'll also learn from the ways people have always pushed back against this violence. We will consider what relationship anarchy can offer us, such as community care, queer and trans liberation, disability justice, and interconnectedness with our environment.

In Chapter 2, we'll deepen our understanding of the power dynamics that shape our world by focusing on how social norms have shaped us as individuals and collectively. We'll ask ourselves how monogamy and marriage have shaped our personal views on relationships, and what is at stake if we choose to push back on these views. We'll consider the diversity of human expression, and learn about the many ways humans build relationships. Nuance will hold us in the space of contradicting desires: We'll consider how we can affirm our authentic and diverse needs as humans as we seek to create a liberated world for all people.

In Chapter 3 we will consider some of the necessary foundations for relationship building, such as understanding our inner attachment world as well as power dynamics between humans. We will start building up our emotional toolbox, learning about somatic tools, shadow work, ancestral support, and pathways to intimacy and connection.

Chapter 4 will guide us into connection with others, offering insight on communication, compatibility, and determining the relationship you want/need with people you love. It is here that we'll embark on building collaborative tools that we can use with other people to build relationships, such as the relationship anarchy smorgasbord, and many prompts to begin deep conversations about what you crave from love.

Chapter 5 honors the dark and messy parts of relationships, inviting us to reckon with fear, rejection, challenges, dealbreakers, conflict, and mistakes. In this chapter you'll be invited to face the shadows that make loving others, and yourself, painful or challenging. As always, we'll ground this journey in compassion and curiosity, practicing our communication when change arises and creating structures that support relationships through conflict.

As we near the end of this book I will invite you to explore the relationship anarchy manifesto with me. With the knowledge and experience we've gained, we'll reflect on this document and bring life to it with our living, breathing, present perspectives. From here, you'll find a resource page full of real humans to connect, organize, and love with. I hope you'll reach out to them, exchange knowledge, and continue this endeavor of love.

CHAPTER 1

What Is Relationship Anarchy and What Can It Offer?

The best things that have ever happened to me have always been just outside the realm of what I thought was possible.

ATIRA (THEY/THEM), AN INTERVIEWEE

I am writing this book because I believe that relationship anarchy is one pathway to greater intimacy, community support, and radically beautiful relationships. Regardless of whether or not people choose to identify as relationship anarchists or practice relationship anarchy, I feel excited to share the knowledge and wisdom learning about relationship anarchy has offered me and others in my community because there are so many ways to love other people.

However we love others, we may find that love and relationships bring challenge, fear, pain, and uncertainty into our lives. Loving each other well is a constant challenge for many of us. In relationships we are tasked with holding the tender bodies of humans with care, knowing that hurt feelings and conflict are inevitable. We do this fragile tending while living on a planet that is harmed and threatened by humans, having formed our first bonds in the oppressive culture of capitalism, white supremacy, and colonialism. Our relationships are impacted by the dominant social structure and environment, and our relationships impact the dominant social structure and environment.

Relationship anarchy is a relational approach that invites an awareness of these realities. It is a philosophy and practical approach to building relationships with others that takes society, environment, culture, *and* love between individuals into account. Relationship anarchy is not just a pathway to love, but a pathway to liberation.

The concept of relationship anarchy was developed from anarchist values. Commonly misunderstood as "chaos," anarchy is simply a rejection of the belief that government is a required facet of thriving human society. As a teenager, I learned about anarchy from my older brother, who was deep in anti-capitalist politics. Hearing my brother describe his interest in anarchy, I immediately had an image of a young white man building bombs in the basement of a high school. I can't place when or where I received the message that anarchists are white supremacist terrorists, but I certainly did. When I took a second to listen and think about it, I realized that it made complete sense that anarchy would be more complex and nuanced than the stereotype I had in my head.

The Anarchist Library, an online resource for anarchist theory and thought, cites Bob Black's "Anarchy 101," from *Defacing the Currency* (2012). Black writes that "the 'bomb-throwing anarchist' stereotype was concocted by politicians and journalists in the late nineteenth century, and they still won't let go of it, but even back then it was a gross exaggeration." Anarchism is more accurately described as a way of relating that relies on voluntary, consent-based cooperation.

There are, of course, different approaches to anarchy. Some anarchists hold the belief that hierarchy between humans is completely unnecessary, while others are more interested in merging certain aspects of current society and past anarchist communities. These are the guiding beliefs of anarchism: we must consent to function in a communal way, we can resolve conflict through mediation and input from everyone in a community, it is not necessary to create systems of power in order to keep peace between people, and people should be able to contribute directly to the decisions that will impact their lives.

In an interview with Andie Nordgren (she/her), one of the foundational thinkers in the development of relationship anarchy, Andie shared with me her perspective on the link between relationship anarchy and anarchist values.

There are all kinds of different feelings that you can have for people that may be the reason that you want more time with them or you want deeper commitments with them, to things like life together or maybe kids together, maybe you buy a house together. But those things can be true without having to organize it by a. this rigid binary and b. the prescribed norms societies regulate. If you listen to them (the binaries and social norms), they kind of dictate that the moment you feel these feelings, then you're supposed to go on the escalator to a more and more committed relationship of a very particular type that is then also normatively supposed to include XY and Z and absolutely not supposed to include some other things because if it does, it's like, invalidated.

So, even if you're in a monogamous committed relationship, if your partner sleeps with somebody else, it's presumably a problem for you. And, so on, even though it may not be at all... That's why for me, the anarchist principle of "if something affects me, I should have a say about it and I should have a say about the rules" [is important]. Not every detail, because you can always use it as a power tactic to say, well, "because I love you, everything you do affects me so I get to control you so that I can make sure I don't feel that like," no, no, no. You don't get to exert a bunch of restrictions on the other person's agency just to manage your own feelings. That's not what relationship anarchy tells you. But, if we want to give each person agency and influence over the agreements that govern your relationship, then you can't just non consensually [and] completely change the agreement.

Now, the problem in this space, is that, of course, the established relationships form love or friendship or whatever give you a shorthand for what to expect, just like in the theater. You know the room, with how the seats are organized and the stage and so on, it gives you framing for what to expect. And if you don't see any other signals, you're gonna expect the normal, right? And so one of the challenges with rejecting those defaults is that it takes a lot of work to make your own. And this is one of the challenges that I've grown to see. Something that I think people need to think about when they enter these types of relationships is that preexisting power dynamics kind of follow into that work. So, if you're gonna open up and say, okay, nothing applies, we're just gonna kind of negotiate a new agreement, you don't come naked into that conversation, right? You come with existing privilege, you have the whole question of epistemic justice. Like, who gets to even define concepts or how we describe reality? Who gets to be a reliable narrator of their own situation knowledge or what's important?

Andie helps us understand that while anarchy is a process of destabilizing hierarchy and norms, we can't leave our relationships unattended after this process of destabilization. She posits that if we don't replace previous dynamics with new approaches to relating, we will simply replicate the power dynamics that were initially present. This is why it can be so difficult to develop communities and relationships outside our existing power structures. We inevitably find ourselves falling back into old patterns and the status quo.

S (she/her), a lesbian polyamorous person, described how an uninterrogated monogamous hierarchy mindset impacted her first polyamorous relationship:

> Because I was new to the concept of polyamory, I hadn't experienced any of it. So in my head, I thought I was a secondary partner because [my partner and my metamour[1]] have been friends for more than ten years and after that they started dating. I was okay with that, I was prepared. I was like, okay, this person [my metamour] is important. It's a priority. And I'm also coming from a very monogamous structure. So, I had that in mind.
>
> There was this one time that I was pretty low and I called [my partner] and when she got the call she said she was talking to her other partner and I said, "Okay, cool, cool." And then she called later, she realized that I was low and she was like, "Why didn't you tell me? I would have cut the call because you needed the attention at that time." So I was like, "But you were talking to them and I feel like it doesn't work like that." Like, there's no hierarchy if all relationships are equal. So, we had a long discussion and I understood, I said,

---

1   Your partner's partner.

okay, that makes sense. Like every relationship will have that respect at whatever capacity it's going or evolving at. And I feel like the more I thought about it, the more I experienced it, I realized hierarchy kind of contradicts because then you're not organically letting the connection also flow.

S and her partner revealed a point of misunderstanding in their relationship. S was operating with a set of assumptions about how and when she would get given care as a "secondary partner," yet her partner had a different set of expectations for when and how her partners received care. They had to collaboratively build something new by clarifying the terms of the relationship for both of them. These misunderstandings are bound to happen, because we can't read each other's minds. We all have a unique set of experiences and knowledge that undergird how we make sense of the world. We invariably come up against our differences.

The people who are most impacted by violent social norms are often most compelled to transform these systems and replace them with something better. Black, Brown, Indigenous, queer, trans, neurodivergent, disabled, and people "othered" in all manners have sought to develop a praxis for relationships that is in opposition to the violence and coercion undergirding white supremacist cis hetero patriarchal western society. This resistance is how the term relationship anarchy came to be. A "Masterclass" article on relationship anarchy reports that, "Queer feminist Andie Nordgren coined 'relationship anarchy' in a 2006 pamphlet that was later widely circulated online on a Swedish website under the title 'The Short Instructional Manifesto for Relationship Anarchy'" (Masterclass 2023). However, it is clear that relationship anarchy did not form from one person, but from a communal process of questioning binaries. Andie explains:

> Queer feminism was always at the center of the project because once you question the gender binary, then you start to, by definition, question the sexuality definitions. And when you're questioning the sexuality definitions, now you're also questioning the relationship definitions because what defines a relationship when you're blurring and queering both the gender and sexuality binaries? Then why not stick it to the other big binary in the room here which is love/not love?

Relationship anarchy is a deconstruction of a love/not love binary. In white, western society, romantic relationships are considered the nexus of love, while all other relationships are diminished in their capacity for real love. Relationship anarchy, at its core, is a process of resisting binaries and non-consensual constraints on human expression.

Andie goes on to explain that this deconstruction of binaries was explored in live action role-playing games that she and her community played.

> The other entry point is really coming out of this participation focused art practice. I'm still a part of the community in the Nordics working with live action role-playing games and participation-driven art where the design material is the agreements between people about how to treat things. So, in live action role-playing games, that's the medium that you work in, right? It's coming up with new games... There's a magic circle that defines, what's inside the game, what's outside the game and which layers of reality are you changing the

rules in? Like, you can play fight in the game. But as soon as you punch someone for real, you've like punched through the magic circle...and...everybody drops out of the game, right?

Relationship anarchy was born from play. It is from the collaborative material of art and play that this concept emerged. It is interesting, therefore, to consider that while Andie is often named as the creator of this term, she herself reported that development of the term "relationship anarchy" was a communal process. How (and why) do we place ownership on an idea that spans across human experience? How do we reconcile the popularized use of this term with the many other terms and descriptions of relationship anarchy that may have come before or speak more accurately to the project (such as Indigenous approaches to relationships)? I encourage you not to hold tightly to the term "relationship anarchy," as there will certainly come a time when this phrase no longer accurately expresses the inherent shape-shifting of this relationship style.

Relationship anarchy is a practice of subversion. Always returning to the people, not the structure, relationship anarchy invites us to consider how things impact us and what we'd like to do with that impact. This is why when I interviewed people for this book I focused less on the specific terms they used for their relationships and more on the approach they took to relationships. Identifying as a relationship anarchist is not a requirement for practicing something that could be described as relationship anarchy. In fact, rejecting the labels and terms of something to tailor it for your needs is perhaps the most relationship anarchist thing you can do! The term "relationship anarchy" may become completely obsolete in the near future, and that's okay, because the underlying values of relationship anarchy are transformative.

For many people, relationship anarchy is related to their practice of non-monogamy. In this book we discuss non-monogamy quite a bit, but relationship anarchy is not inherently non-monogamous. It is possible to be monogamous and a relationship anarchist. That being said, monogamy that is also relationship anarchy is an inherently non-normative monogamy. The same way that men carry patriarchy with them and white people carry white supremacy, monogamous relationships carry the historical and structural history of coercive monogamy. That doesn't mean that all monogamy is coercive. If you are monogamous, you are welcome here. I have no secret agenda to change the number of people that you date or partner with. In fact, I feel very invested in people doing whatever is right for them. However, I would encourage you to consider that the way you approach your monogamy may change after reading this book. Relationship anarchy is a relationship style that challenges what we know, encourages us to deconstruct social norms, and lives in the rejection of fixed definitions and determinations. This inherent shape-shifting is what I have come to love most about those who practice relationship anarchy. Kim Tallbear (2016) explains:

> [N]on-monogamous people also often privilege sexual relating in their definitions of what constitutes ethical non-monogamy, or plural loves. Might we have great loves that don't involve sex? Loves whom we do not compartmentalize into friend versus lover, with the word "just" preceding "friends"? Most of the great loves of my life are humans who I do or did not relate to sexually. They include my closest family members, and also a man who I have had sexual desire for, but that is not the relationship it is possible for us to have. I love him without regret. We have never been physically intimate. Is this

somehow a "just" friends relationship? I do not love him less than the people I have been "in love" with. Might we also not have great and important loves that do not even involve other humans, but rather vocations, art, and other practices?

While non-monogamy is ripe with possibilities for liberation, it is equally possible to inhabit a non-monogamous relationship that is coercive and imbalanced. Some non-monogamous folks develop a shadowy story that being non-monogamous is more evolved, inherently "human," or loving. I have certainly felt this feeling before, especially as I started my non-monogamous journey and faced so many barriers to support and understanding. A way to make sense of my experience of social rejection was to declare that non-monogamous people had come up with a better way that everyone else just hadn't discovered yet. This mindset sought to protect me from the hurt of feeling ostracized by mainstream society and many of my close family and friends. But, non-monogamy is not inherently better. It is an approach to relationships. One of those approaches that lives in the expansive soup of being *not* something else. There are so many ways to not be monogamous, which means there are so many ways to fuck up, thrive, and just get by non-monogamously. As you read this book, I invite you to explore how relationship anarchy might change your practice of your relationships, whether non-monogamous, monogamous, or a secret third thing. Where do you find the edges of your relational boundaries? What lives in the discomfort of surrender? What kind of liberation might come from releasing claims on others?

I invite you to pause for a moment as you read these words: How does it feel in your body to be reading this book so far? Are you excited to learn more, anxious to read on, or feeling your attention wavering? What colors, shapes, or sensations might describe your inner world? (You can draw them!) Do you feel numbness or nothingness? Do you notice thoughts moving through your head?

Andie Nordgren and her queer anarchist community gave us the gift of the term "relationship anarchy," but it is a practice that extends farther past 2006. Since humans have existed, we have been required to create meaningful relationships with other humans to survive. These connections have been the glue of human society and a necessary ingredient in human survival. It is within relationships that we've been able to find food, raise children, create art, survive plagues, protect each other from harm, and experience the joy of human connection. It is only recently in human history that there has been a prioritization of romantic relationships over all others. As Sue Johnson shares in *Hold Me Tight*, "Inevitably, we now ask our lovers for the emotional connection and sense of belonging that my grandmother could get from a whole village" (2008, p.15).

In an episode of the podcast, "All My Relations," Kim Tallbear reframes "non-monogamous" practices outside of white, settler-colonial embodiment (Wilbur and Keene 2019). She explains how although she doesn't know the terms and exact practices of her ancestors, it is possible to track the traces of the way people created "good relations," which offers a guide for how to treat other people with respect, dignity, and mutuality, rather than as objects that can be owned, bought, or traded. I highly recommend listening to this section of the podcast while you read the transcript.[2]

---

2 www.allmyrelationspodcast.com/post/ep-5-decolonizing-sex; the conversation quoted starts at about 30 minutes and 20 seconds in, but I highly recommend listening to the whole episode.

I do look for the traces or the stories that are there about how [my ancestors] did live outside of these structures that we now take for granted, you know?... So I would like us to sort of, I guess, what I advocate is, that we take the fundamental ethical frameworks of our ancestors, that we have retained, one of which I think is this notion of being in "good relation," and we figure out how, how do we think through that in relationship to our intimate relationships too? So for me, being in "good relation" and looking at the way that my ancestors shared resources, the way that they shared childcare, the way that say somebody would take on extra wives (you know, if they needed to be taken into a family). We don't know if they had sex or not and it's not our business... In fact, we know by most long-term marriages they're pretty sexless, so marriage and sex do not go together for very long so who cares. It's about taking care of family, it's about taking care of each other... I just think there was less, kind of, ownership of the individual body... I find this, kind of, exercising territoriality over land, and over somebody else's body and desire, I just find that immoral, and I will not do it... I don't know that there's a precedence for that in our, in our ancestors' ways of being, I just don't see it if I look at their fundamental ways of trying to think about being in relation. I would view a contemporary sexual relationship [and] I would like to articulate it with that idea as much as possible, not with ownership ideas.

Knowing that many people have been practicing relationships in an equitable way for much longer than settler colonialism has existed, how do we bring this knowledge into the present without divorcing ourselves from the circumstances through which we've arrived here? In my interview with

Seán (they/them) (nêhi(th/y)aw/otipemisiwak/Nakawé/
Irish), they shared with me a question often discussed in their
community: Is it possible to truly consent on stolen land?
This question is important because it highlights the history of
violence that undergirds every interaction we have with one
another, especially in what today is known as the Americas,
or as Turtle Island to many Indigenous communities. This
perspective illuminates the importance of repair, transformation, and change as we move forward together. We cannot
simply strip away the current norms without replacing them
without something else, nor can we barrel into new ways of
being without acknowledging how we arrived there and doing
the necessary repair to begin recovery. While some of us may
not carry in our bodies the active trauma of having our land
and culture stolen in ongoing ways, it is an aspect of our world
that impacts us all. We must find ways to reckon with the
impact of our experiences on our relationships. Part of this
journey is bringing what we carry to the forefront, naming it,
honoring it, and asking: How can we tend to this?

How do you like to be tended to so that your history,
your present self, and your future iterations can be held in
a relationship? What makes you feel seen, understood, and
acknowledged?

Consider: Is there space in your relationships for political
engagement and social justice? What do you notice in your
body when you think about incorporating social justice into
your interpersonal relationships? Have you ever gone to a
protest with someone you love or had a hard conversation
about inequity? What are these experiences like for you?

Relationship anarchy is a balm to individualism and isola-
tion. It is a return to our human need to care for others and
be cared for ourselves. It is a reminder that we are valuable;

regardless of what we can offer to capitalism, our bodies matter.

Relationship anarchy offers us chosen family, expansive romance, diverse connections, and intimate friendships. These things can benefit all of us, regardless of our identities, but they are especially transformative for those of us who have been denied love, connection, or community because of our identities.

For many queer people, the idea of a chosen family has become a crucial part of queer survival and queer joy, but this concept can be transformative for anyone. Cis-hetero-patriarchal society is also harmful to those who most effectively fit the "ideal" of what a person, or people, should be. Being marginalized is harmful, but being queer, and being offered a perspective of relationships outside of the norm, is a gift. We can learn so many lessons from non-normative communities and experiences. Straight and cisgender people can also benefit from these lessons if they are open to the gift of queer love and experiences.

In 2023 artist and activist Alok Vaid Menon was a guest on "Man Enough," a podcast that explores how gender roles affect men and all people in current society (see Yurcaba 2021). Alok shared their perspective on why so many people are resistant to receiving the wisdom of genderqueer love and embodiment.

> I don't think the majority of people are ready to heal, and that's why they repress us as trans and gender-variant people—because they've done this violence to themselves first. They've repressed their own femininity. They've repressed their own gender nonconformity. They've repressed their own ambivalence. They've repressed their own creativity.

Non-normative humans reflect the worst fears of those who conform to society's expectations: being true to yourself, being authentic, being loud, bright, or gorgeous in front of others despite the threat of judgment, ridicule, or harm. Our society espouses the belief that we must conform in order to experience connection and love. Many of us are punished implicitly and explicitly for expressing ourselves. When we choose to break the rules, we activate fear that the rules don't matter.

Many of the people I interviewed for this book expressed the same anxiety: Is it possible that I could be accepted, loved, and supported just as I am? And, without relying on legal marriage and widespread social acceptance, will my relationships still matter? These two questions speak to two pervasive fears in our society. One, that we may never be accepted as our true selves by others. And two, that without the constrictive social norms, relationships and connection will be meaningless. These anxieties make sense! Embarking on non-normative pathways is scary. Without clear social scripts, there is a lot of room for confusion and uncertainty.

In her book *Polysecure*, Jessica Fern writes that consensual non-monogamy "is a relationship structure that is inherently insecure" (2020, p.74). The reality that relationships of all kinds can activate our nervous systems is undeniable. But why would a relationship style that is rooted in community care, consent, autonomy, and authentic support be so triggering for so many of us? These seem like good things that anyone and everyone might strive for! We know that humans benefit from both connection and autonomy in appropriate doses. And yet, when offered the freedom of self-expression that relationship anarchy espouses, many of us feel panic.

When interviewing Seán, they spoke to me about the longevity of expansive relationality in their communities. They described relations as "Treaty:" mutual agreements between people about how to navigate rupture, repair, and daily care. Seán told me about histories of Indigenous communities creating mutually supportive, nuanced, and complex kinship relationships since time immemorial. They described relationship anarchy as most closely translated to "wâhkôhtowin," a conceptual framework of kinship in Cree that emphasizes all relationships as valuable, including our relationships with spirit, animal, nature, and other non-human entities. Seán emphasized that their personal relationship to wâhkôhtowin and/or relationship anarchy is deeply rooted in decolonization. They posed the question: What does it mean to have good relations? Perhaps one feature of having good relations is embracing the challenging feelings that come up when in relationships, such as fear, sadness, anxiety, and hurt.

Seán made clear connections between the political and socio-cultural experience of their life and their interpersonal connections. They described how being in relationship with settlers poses unique challenges. When I asked Seán what they wish they knew before they started their relationship anarchy/poly/relationship journey, they responded: "I wish I knew how some of these power imbalances would factor in." This sentiment reminded me of the impact an environment of trauma, both interpersonal and cultural, has on our nervous systems. Existing in a post-colonial, capitalist, white supremacist world is inherently traumatic. Of course relationships would be activating, when western society is founded on betrayal, violence, and abuse between people!

In western society, our value is tied to our ability to participate in capitalism. This culture leads to a constant and pervasive anxiety that nothing will ever be enough. There is no end point, no rest, no final day of work until we die. Our relationships are impacted by this culture. Many of us consciously and subconsciously see people as either valuable to capitalism or unimportant. We are trained from a young age to consume and hoard as much wealth as possible. Sometimes called a "scarcity mindset," capitalism teaches us that there is not enough for everyone, when that is actually not true. This scarcity mindset influences our relationships. We may feel that there is never enough love, time, energy, or care. This feeling can be very real, as for many of us, there isn't enough time to get our needs met because we constantly have to override our physical and emotional needs in order to work. However, it is also possible to resist a scarcity mindset by asking for help, collaborating with others on how to get our needs met, and taking responsibility for meeting our own needs, instead of expecting others to do it without us asking them. This doesn't mean that we don't need others in order to get our needs met, but that the responsibility of asking for connection, help, and reassurance lies squarely in our own bodies. Towards the end of our interview, Seán shared some wise advice: "Don't treat people like resources, treat people like kin." To me, this encompasses this decolonial and anti-capitalist view of relationships. We may not realize how deeply embedded capitalism is in our relationships until we start to untangle ourselves from them.

Can you give an example of a way you might treat someone like a resource? How would it be different to treat someone like kin? What does it feel like to you when someone treats you more like a resource or more like kin?

Capitalism and white supremacy also influence our beliefs about who is a desirable partner. Disability justice activists and scholars have discussed this extensively, illustrating the way disabled folks are considered to be less desirable partners if they cannot participate in capitalism to the same capacity as able-bodied people. We see this in the cultural idea that a good partner is able to provide care whenever we need it, offer money, resources, real estate, and social status. Imagine for a moment that everyone was provided with adequate food, shelter, water, and access to play. Would a certainty that your basic needs are met change who you pursued as a partner in life? What if you were able to ensure those needs were met— how would you want to spend your time?

But we still live in a capitalist society, and so we must grapple with the realities of surviving our current world. Marginalized people continue to seek assimilation into dominant culture because this is one way to survive. A great example of this is the pursuit of marriage equality for LGBTQ+ couples. In her book *Liberated to the Bone*, Susan Raffo beautifully explains how the pursuit of legal marriage rights for queer people was actually an effective effort to destabilize the intersectional movements between Black and queer people forming to address all manner of relational inequality, disability rights, white supremacy, and structural inequality:

> The marriage fight created wedges in LGBTQ communities. Wedges between generations, between flavors and shapes of queerness. One of the wedges was a conflict between different approaches to change. Whether you felt invisibilized by the inability to marry or you felt invisibilized by the demand for marriage equality, there was stress, harm, and overt and indirect violence unfolding, and what resulted is what the brain does when in power struggle moments. The choices seemed to be either submit or defy. (Raffo 2022, p.173)

This is not to say that you can't authentically desire marriage, but rather that many of us feel explicitly or implicitly coerced to prioritize marriage in our lives because it upholds the status quo. We may feel explicitly coerced when friends or family ask us repeatedly when we're going to get married, show the most interest in our lives when we are dating someone, or state that our wedding day will be the happiest day of our life. We may feel implicitly coerced when we see that everyone around us is getting married, when unmarried partnerships don't receive financial benefits, or when people get silent if we bring up a non-normative relationship style.

White supremacy is at the root of these inequities. It is one of the greatest influences on our relational world. It undergirds the power dynamics between people at all levels of society. James Baldwin wrote, "History is not the past, it is the present. We carry our history with us. We are our history" (Baldwin and Peck 2017, p.138). To honor our past we must carry it with us in our present through active remembering, listening to those who lived through formative moments in history, and committing to change in the future when we see harmful patterns emerge. Our human history lives in the relational present of our bodies, the love, connection, and meaning we make between each other. Our history also lives in our limitations for love and connection, and the way we deny the humanity of Black, Brown, and Indigenous humans. When exploring non-normative relationship approaches like relationship anarchy, it is imperative that we keep our embodied experience of power close to our conversations, because the social dynamics of power are expressed through our bodies. In *My Grandmother's Hands: Racialized Trauma and the Pathway to Mending Our Hearts and Bodies* Resmaa Menakem writes that "for the most part, white supremacy lives in our bodies.

In fact, white supremacy would be better termed white-body supremacy, because every white-skinned body, no matter who inhabits it—and no matter what they think, believe, do, or say—automatically benefits from it" (2017, p.16). Menakem emphasizes the importance of identifying how our physical bodies are experienced in social and communal exchange. The shape, color, form, composition, neural pathways, and sensory experiences of our bodies are impacted by our racialized experiences. In order to discuss relationship anarchy we must reckon with the power dynamics that influence and form our human relationships.

One way we can begin to reckon with these dynamics is through engagement with the way white supremacy impacts our daily lives. Many of you reading this know and embody these truths by virtue of living in Black, Brown, and/or Indigenous bodies. For the white people reading this, let this be an invitation to beginnings. It is not possible to discuss relationships without discussing the fabric of power that impacts relationships. But, these conversations, and more importantly the actions that come from conversations, must persist throughout our lives beyond this moment. In *Dismantling Racism: A Workbook for Social Change Groups* (2001), Kenneth Jones and Tema Okun articulate the many features of white supremacist culture that we may not even associate with whiteness. Some of these features (and I'm sure there are many more to be named) are perfectionism, sense of urgency, defensiveness, quantity over quality, worship of the written word, paternalism, power hoarding, fear of open conflict, individualism, progress is bigger and more, objectivity, and right to comfort. This is also a list of things that make loving, equitable relationships difficult to form. It is necessary as we embark on deep relational work to identify the ways whiteness and white supremacy are being replicated in our interpersonal worlds.

How does white supremacy impact your relationships? In what ways do you protect your body, well-being and peace from violence from other humans? Who can be trusted? How do you embark on building intimacy with those who hold more or less privilege than you?

We live in a moment of immense denial of the ways our white supremacist culture is violent. Even in the spaces that strive for equity we come up against the violence of whiteness. In their essay "The Gap: Social Wounds and Personal Transformation," Tayla Shanae describes an experience of witnessing an activist community come up against the internal system of whiteness that is present in this community:

> ...in one Earth connection-based gathering, there was an entire day dedicated to telling an indigenous tale about the importance of the role of the healer in creating a healthy village. At the same time, the storytellers were not attending to the fact that the gathering itself was composed of a largely white and middle-class community adapting indigenous skills to build this village. As one of the only women of color in the gathering, I could feel a tension growing in me that the clear lack of accessibility and welcoming to brown and black people was not being addressed in a gathering dedicated to building diversity and creating a village. (Shanae 2018, p.275)

Shanae speaks to the way good intentions can get in the way of authentic connection and change. Shanae was aware of the disconnection between intention (honoring indigenous storytelling) and the impact on their lived experience as a woman of color (feeling tension as they became aware of the lack of accessibility to Black and Brown people). A desire to transform our relationships does not guarantee transformation.

Western society is so steeped in violence, disregard of consent, purity culture, perfectionism, and the desire to maintain power that these themes interplay with all our relationships. We unknowingly create relationships founded on ownership and hidden expectations, rather than autonomy and co-created connections. We mistake rules for boundaries, and we subtly coerce people to stay in our life even when they want to leave. We ignore or repress our true feelings for fear of being expelled or marginalized further. We silence each other in order to maintain the status quo. Artist and DJ Aloiso Wilmoth said in an interview, "Isn't it weird how the same people that always talk about dismantling the police, or prison abolition, then turn around and act like the police?" (Blue 2022).

This is not how humans have always existed, and not how many humans exist now. Throughout history Indigenous and colonized peoples have resisted colonial frameworks of relationships. Practices of non-monogamy and polyamory have been embodied as a pathway of resistance to oppressive ideologies throughout history and today. Ximena (they/them), a trans Argentinian who has identified as polyamorous and a relationship anarchist through their life, shared with me the way relationship anarchist values were incorporated into their upbringing.

I guess what might be also relevant is my cultural background. I'm actually from Argentina and I moved to the US when I was eleven. Even though my parents would never identify with any of the words that I use for any of these things, including the words "chosen family," the examples that I had were that my parents were definitely each other's circle, but my family or the presence around me was much broader than that and it was much more communal. I grew up with my grandmother's kindergarten friends around me. Those were folks that I saw, my mom has been friends with the same people since she was in kindergarten. And those are people that I would probably call "chosen family" who are essentially like aunts and uncles, kids I grew up with, you know?

So I feel like I don't have this idea that I have seen in the US a lot or at least historically with my partners where your romantic partner is number one and even blood family comes second. And certainly all other non-blood relationships then come third. And I have a nephew who's chosen family, well their whole family is chosen family. But I've known my nephew since before he was born and we have an incredibly close relationship. One of my exes would regularly be like, "that's not your nephew. Like you're not related to them. I should still come first." And those were just things that I never aligned with, not just when it comes to chosen family, but also my friends and the way that I think about prioritizing care for the people that I love. And this idea that a romantic partner should always come first in one way or another [shaking head]. Because I always was like, I mean you are really important to me or I wouldn't choose to be sharing my life with you in this way. And also there's so many other people in my life who are also very important and I could never possibly compare one over the other no matter how long or how short or how big or how small those relationships were.

People who love each other in a relationship anarchy kind of way may not use the term relationship anarchy to describe their relationships and that's okay. Relationship anarchy, as a practice, encourages everyone to create and use terms that work best for them. A relationship anarchy approach is simply an approach that prioritizes people over systems.

In order to understand the kinds of relationships we want to have we must understand the conditioning we've received about what kinds of relationships matter. Western society has built up a specific belief system, one that is taught through school, family, friendships, social structures, work, and romantic relationships. This belief system espouses that white, cisgender, heterosexual, monogamous, romantic marriages are ideal, and anything else isn't worth much. We learn from a young age that we must conform to certain expectations to receive connection. As children this is paramount, because without this connection to our caregivers, we would literally die. We are faced with the task of identifying how much of our authentic self we can express without being ostracized by the humans that keep us safe. For many of us, marriage is a crucial element of our first relationship landscape: the way we first came to understand how humans connect. Even if your parents weren't married or you grew up in a family that didn't believe in the importance of marriage, marriage is considered by many to be paramount to a healthy society and to being a healthy human.

The emphasis on romantic marriage in the twentieth century can be illustrated by countless books, movies, and TV shows that glorify and celebrate romantic marriage as the goal of all romantic relationships. Sue Johnson writes that:

> ...movies as well as television soap operas and dramas saturate us with images of romantic love as the be-all and end-all of relationships, while newspapers, magazines, and TV news avidly report on the never-ending search for romance and

love among actors and celebrities. So, it should come as no surprise that people recently surveyed in the US and Canada rate a satisfying love relationship as their number-one goal, ahead of financial success and satisfying career. (2008, p.15)

How many romantic movies have you seen that *end* with marriage? As if a relationship transitions into blissful marital joy the moment you tie the knot. Everywhere you look there are explicit and implicit messages that marriage is the best thing you can do for yourself.

Growing up I remember my parents talking at length about their single friends, wondering if they would ever get married or find a partner. As a kid, I understood that being single was "bad," and "scary." At thirteen I was terrified I would never be in love, never get married, and be alone forever. These three things were inseparable in my mind. If you don't fall in love, I reasoned, you can't get married, and if you don't get married, you'll be sad, lonely, and pathetic. There was a clear binary: Marriage equals love and single equals lonely.

The social privilege and status that married and some long-term couples enjoy is called "couples privilege." Juan-Carlos Pérez-Cortés explains couples privilege as "how automatically legible a relationship is in terms of emotional and life importance without the need for further clarification" (2020, p.52). I think of couples privilege as all the implicit and explicit assumptions we make about couples that prioritize and legitimize their relationship in the eyes of others. Even if we don't individually subscribe to the hierarchy of romantic couples over other kinds of partnerships, the belief that romantic couples are a more normal and valid way to relate and the structural privileges that come with that belief (such as legal marriage) permeates the relational landscape we all navigate.

We will deepen our understanding of couples privilege, and the power differentials at play in all relationships in Chapter 3 of this book when we dive into the way we can practically construct our relationships.

For this book, I interviewed several people who were legally married or married by commitment. Many of them spoke to the logistic value of marrying a partner in our society. Many of them also named the importance of marriage in their social and cultural world. A defining thread in the stories of everyone I interviewed was an intentional assessment of the benefits and costs of being legally married. This kind of intentionality is often a requirement for queer and/or disabled people. It is often said that in the US we achieved marriage equality when gay marriage was legalized in in all states in 2015. However, for many disabled folks getting legally married would require them to give up essential social services. Does marriage equality really exist if disabled folks can't be married and also survive?

This prioritization of marriage started with a cultural requirement for segregated, monogamous marriage, an important tool in the project of white supremacy and colonialism. Marriage was not initially associated with romance; it was a way to bond families so they could share resources. These resources included land, animals, tools, and money as well as humans who could bear and raise children. In the US, marriage was a privilege afforded to those with more power and status, so that they could acquire and keep more resources. The marriages of enslaved people were not recognized by US law.

It became essential in US white communities to restrict people from marrying outside their race. If white and Black people were able to relate, connect, and marry, it would be harder to control these rigid social lines of race. In an episode on the podcast "At Liberty" (Murray 2019) Melissa Murray explains how central marriage was to maintain white supremacy from the beginning of chattel slavery. She explains that in the seventeenth century, slavery was a matrilineal process. Thus, "if your mother is free, you're born free. If your mother is enslaved, you too, are enslaved. And so this creates enormous problems if you have free white women either marrying or having relationships with Black men who are enslaved or free." Murray makes the point that marriage between white and Black people was also influenced by intersections of race and gender. It is not an accident that the well-known case of Loving v. Virginia, that was the catalyst for removing anti-miscegenation laws across the US, was the case of a Black woman and a white man. Five years before Loving v. Virginia, there was another case called McLaughlin v. Florida which features a Black man and a white woman. Murray explains that "part of the reason why it doesn't live large in our legal imagination is because the two people are much more contro-versial in terms of who they represent."

As you can see, the institution of marriage has been hard at work to control and confine the way people relate. Roman-tic love became incorporated into our idea of marriage quite recently. Romantic love wasn't necessary for the exchange of resources, but it became an incredibly valuable way to main-tain the supremacy of marriage. As Enlightenment thinkers began to espouse ideas of "right to personal happiness," and slavery, economic development, and industrialization made material wealth more accessible for white individuals, the historic reasons for marriage (material exchange and familial duty) became less resonant. Romantic love became a romantic solution: a way to incorporate individual emotional expression into a system that maintains social order. Stephanie Coontz writes, "People have always fallen in love, and throughout the ages many couples have loved each other deeply. But only rarely in history has love been seen as the main reason for getting married. When someone did advocate such a strange belief, it was no laughing matter. Instead it was considered a serious threat to social order" (Coontz 2016).

In the present day, marriage offers able-bodied, cisgender, heterosexual people social and material resources that are otherwise inaccessible. In an enlightening dissertation on the ways marriage protects white supremacy, Katharine Franks Kyros (2011) writes:

> Miscegenation laws were used to target and punish individuals engaging in relationships that threatened the social order. The exclusion of same-sex couples from marriage reinforces the image of the homosexual as an outsider, drawing upon a long history of marginalization and othering. Same-sex couples denied the right to legally marry face denial of inheritance of property and wealth, denial of hospital visitation rights, limits to adopting or gaining custody of children, as well as roughly 1,135 other rights afforded to heterosexual married couples.

Many people today opt to get married in order to access tax benefits, healthcare, rights to information when a partner is ill, custody of children, shared resources and money, and more. Marriage is a huge structural part of Western society. The pressure to get married, and to conform, is present in the psyches and bodies of many people living in this part of the world.

For now, let's consider some of our values and biases about romantic relationships and marriage. Take a pause here to consider the following questions. I invite you to talk out loud as you respond to these questions, either to yourself or to a friend.

- What kinds of messages did you get about monogamy and non-monogamy growing up?
- Did you grow up in a religious or cultural tradition that prioritized marriage? What did you learn was valuable about getting married?
- What did you learn growing up about the roles of men and women in marriages?
- Do you feel the desire to get married? Why or why not?
- What are the important qualities of a marriage?

What non-romantic relationships are valuable in your life? Can non-romantic relationships be as important or more important than a romantic married relationship? To further understand the landscape of our minds and social encounters, we must also dive into the complexities of how gender is related to romantic relationships in our society. Gender roles are an important facet of maintaining a white supremacist culture. Despite what we are often taught, the existence of "men," and "women," in human cultures is not inherent or universal. The corresponding roles applied to these genders are even more variable. In the book *The Invention of Women*, Oyèrónké Oyěwùmí explores the development of a legible gender category of "woman" in Yoruba culture after Yoruba people first were exposed to Western colonialism and white supremacy. Oyěwùmí explains that determining gender roles based on physical traits was not an aspect of Yoruba society "prior to the infusion of Western notions into Yoruba culture" (1997, p.x). Oyĕwùmí lays out very clearly for us the ways her "analysis challenges a number of ideas...common in many Western feminist writings" (p.xi).

Oyĕwùmí's summary of the ways she challenges western views on gender roles and norms is an extremely helpful mirror for us to understand Western social values. In particular, she challenges the Western idea that "Gender categories are universal and timeless and have been present in every society at all times" (p.xi). By challenging this idea with evidence that alternative gender experiences have existed throughout history, Oyĕwùmí invites us to consider that Western views of gender may not be as monolithic and stagnant as we are led to believe in the West. Oyĕwùmí also challenges the western idea that "the subordination of women is a universal" (p.xii). Without erasing the ways in which women have been subordinated through history, we can use this insight to garner hope that women's role of submission and silence in Western society need not be the path forward. We have an opportunity to create dynamics between humans that feel good to everyone involved, and we can start that process in the relational space of one person with another.

The insights Oyĕwùmí makes about western gender categories are essential to understanding why relationship anarchy is intricately intertwined with non-normative gender, sexuality, and relationships, as well as neurodivergence, disability, Blackness, Indigeneity, and all marginalized identities. What many of us find when exploring one non-normative realm of society is that the other realms of our lives start to be pulled into question too. This was illustrated by Jibril (he/they), a Black non-binary person who shared with me their experience of realizing that there was more nuance and diversity in the way they might explore relationships. I asked them, when did you start to question the status quo? Jibril shared:

> It started probably when I was a kid, watching my parents, and just relationships in general. One of the things I heard growing up from adults was that adults can't be friends with their kids. And my dad has, for my entire life, practically been my best friend. So that was one of those first things where, as a kid observing relationships around me, I started to notice people would say something about something and then I would look at it, I'd go, "but that's not quite true though because my experience is different than what you claim is the 'thing'...that's not lining up. Why isn't that lining up?"

From a young age Jibril had the experience of incongruence with what he knew about himself and the people around him and what those people were saying about what was possible. They knew that their dad was their friend, and yet people said adults couldn't be friends with their kids. How could both be true? As Jibril felt into this discomfort, more inconsistencies began to arise. He continued:

> I also noticed that when these things would happen to other people their reaction was, "But if it doesn't work that way, then it doesn't work at all." But, I felt like I had the direct opposite reaction where I would see it and I would go, "Well, if it doesn't work that way, who says that it has to work that way?" Maybe there's a different way it can work.

When Jibril was telling me this story I found myself wondering, why is it that some of us ask, like Jibril, if there is a different way and some of us try to bury this question?

I invite you to hold this question in your mind and body as you continue reading. How and why do we choose to push against the status quo? As a pansexual, non-binary person who was best friends with his dad, Jibril knew from a young age that the way the world functioned was not reflective of the way his inner world blossomed. Jibril's world was expansive, creative, and complex. He had an innate awareness that things around him could be the same. Being confronted with this discontinuity, Jibril has had to choose whether to conform to society's expectations or to build an external world that reflects their inner world. Jibril continues to grapple with this tension today.

What we can take from Jibril's story is that while we may be heavily shaped by social norms, we also have an incredible capacity as humans to think outside of the box. There are countless ways we can begin to unravel and explore the messages we've been taught throughout our lives. Have there been formative moments in your life in which you challenged the views of your family or culture? Or perhaps a time you felt a commitment to the social structure you were offered? How do you feel about these moments? Who or what were pivotal to them?

Throughout history, trans, non-binary, and gender diverse people have been forced to live non-normative lives in secret. Queer and trans people already exist in non-normative relationships because we exist outside of one of the most legible kinds of relationship: heterosexual romantic love. Just as Jibril described the way representation of a woman having sexual desire disrupted his entire view of relationships, experiencing queer desire disrupts our understanding of what relationships are and can be. Think about the social desire to make sense of queer relationships through a heterosexual lens. Recently

I was touring a potential rental house with one of my partners. After giving us an appraising look, the landlord leaned in nervously and asked us, "So who cooks and who cleans?"

As humans, we want to make sense of things. If all we are offered is heterosexual then we will assume heterosexual is the most normal. There is so little understanding of how queer relationships form, thrive, and function that many queer folks experience a persistent mis-attunement from the world around them. I am reminded of my work at a crisis call center for domestic violence and sexual assault survivors. Most of our callers were cis women survivors in straight relationships with cis men abusers. These power dynamics were considered easy to identify and straightforward to assess. Whenever we had a queer survivor call about their abuse it became much more challenging to determine who was the "abuser," and who was the "survivor." I worried that the uncertainty we experienced as advocates was deeply detrimental to those we served. I also considered how queer relationships might complicate our assessment of what constitutes abuse. And further, were there cis men survivors being assumed as abusers because of the biases our crisis team held? Without falling back on the inherent power dynamic of cisman over ciswoman, how do we identify harm, impact, and responsibility?

What I hope you are starting to see, or to more deeply reflect on, is that there are already cracks in the system. Perhaps relationship anarchy is not such a new approach, but rather a return to something we've banished in ourselves.

Throughout the twenty-first century, we've seen a shift in mainstream culture. Non-normative relationships such as polyamory, non-monogamy, and platonic partnerships have become more visible. Many younger people are reconnecting with and returning to their Indigenous communities, seeking insight on how to navigate the world from tradition and acknowledging that monogamy and many forms of non-monogamy are being enacted from settler-colonialist ways of being.

Non-monogamy can easily be practiced in violent, coercive ways. There is nothing inherently radical, egalitarian, or liberated about having multiple partners. Kim Tallbear reminds us that relational success has much more to do with reckoning with the deep questions about *how* we exist with other humans ethically (Wilbur and Keene 2019). In order to do that, we have to acknowledge that there is knowledge about how to exist with other humans ethically that has been systematically erased by white settlers all over the world. In the next chapter, we'll continue to explore the impact of white settler colonialism and white supremacy on the way we create and sustain relationships.

We are collectively experiencing the trauma of living in a coercive and non-consensual society, and so it makes sense that embarking into an unknown territory of liberation, consent, autonomy, and mutual respect would be activating. To many, relationship anarchy may seem like something that exists in fantasy land. Is it possible to feel safe? Is it possible to create relationships that support me and my nervous system on my own terms? Is it possible to create something beyond what I have been taught? Every step in the direction of liberation is scary. Our bodies can sense the impending threat of being different. We are witness, in ourselves and others, to the way difference is punished in our society.

So it makes sense that relationship anarchy could be activating and triggering. We are rebuilding relationality. We are creating neural pathways. We are dreaming of something that has been suppressed.

When I'm feeling spiritual and connected to the world around me I feel an innate knowledge of how to be loving towards other humans. I feel aware of our human capacity for change, and of my body's yearning for authentic love. I believe that humans know how to love each other, and that we can find our way back to a love that is rooted in justice, liberation, and collective care. We are practicing here, in this book. Let's continue to embark on this journey of discovery in ourselves and with others.

CHAPTER 2

Uncovering What We've Learned about Relationships

The Value of Friend Love

As a young person, my blueprint for relationships came from my best friendship. Sienna and I met in fifth grade, in Ms Daugherty's class. We bonded on our basketball team and quickly discovered we could make each other laugh so hard we could barely breathe. From the time we were eleven or twelve until the end of high school we were inseparable. We spent most of our waking hours together, and lots of our sleeping hours too. I felt a comfort with Sienna that I had never experienced before: the permission to just be. I felt free to run around, laugh uncontrollably, eat, dance, be messy, get dirty, play, dress up, imagine, and try new things. Sienna understood parts of my soul in a way no one else ever has. She saw into my family dynamics, held me when I cried, and helped me navigate torrents of weird teenage sexual experiences. Many of these sexual experiences were so deeply in contrast to the kind of intimacy I experienced with Sienna. We would regularly shower together, give each other massages, and snuggle before bed. As a teenager, it didn't occur to me that the gentleness we shared might be possible in a sexual or romantic connection. In my mind, friendship was safe and romantic relationships were rife with danger.

Towards the end of my high school days, I started to question the binary I had created in my mind. Most of my sexual and romantic experiences at that time were shallow, unpleasant, and even coercive. I fluctuated between feeling exposed and violated in my sexual connections to feeling loved and cherished in my friendship with Sienna. Why couldn't I have both?

As an openly pansexual person my first thought was definitely: Am I in love with my best friend? I've considered this quite a bit over the years, and I always come back to the same conclusion. Yes, I was definitely in love with my best friend, but not in a romantic or sexual way. My love for Sienna was deep, intense, and special, but it never felt like anything but friendship. When I sat with that reality, something opened in me. Why did it feel like my love for Sienna was less valuable or less meaningful than sexual and romantic connections I had? When people asked me about my first sexual experience, I could state a day and time that my body received penetration. But why did it matter? What about the first time I felt safe enough to tell someone else that I masturbated, despite fear and shame that something was wrong with me? What about the countless times Sienna and I showered together, sharing sacred space in which nudity was just human? What about all the times we revealed our most vulnerable parts and held each other in our pain?

Those experiences prepared me for future love in a way that none of my high school boyfriends could comprehend. So why does it still feel sticky and awkward to name Sienna as one of my true loves? The social pressure to reserve love for romance has stuck its sharp fingers so deep into my body that I'm still finding open wounds. I hope that this book and the many educators, therapists, healers, friends, families, and lovers who feel aligned with relationship anarchy will begin to close the wounds of compulsory monogamy and cis-heteronormativity.

What I have found, and what you may find, is that relationships and love are much more complex and nuanced than romantic versus platonic. Andie Nordgren described to me the binary we've created between love/not love. There is an opening and healing that can come from allowing our relationships to develop in their own way, without prescriptive models of how we must be. Sienna and I were lucky to form a relationship that contained many different energies.

There was romance, eroticism, playfulness, re-parenting, teamwork, and partnership all under an umbrella of friendship.

This calls to mind an interaction I had with a friend in college who was intensely attracted to one of their new friends. This friend, Jay, said to me, "I am so attracted to River. I totally want to have sex with them, but I don't want to date them because I'm so busy with school, and I know if we have sex it will ruin our friendship." I remember feeling confused as to why Jay was sure sex would ruin the friendship. He may have been right! But, what if he wasn't? Why does it feel to so many of us that we can't mix sex with friendship? If we follow the thread, what are we truly afraid will happen if we open ourselves up to multiple different energies?

For many people, sex is experienced as an inherently romantic act that comes with certain expectations, agreements, and requirements. Sex can be experienced as something you either do because you love someone or something that is purely physical and unemotional. There is very little discussion in our society about the middle ground between these two opposites. What about sex with someone you like okay but don't love? Or sex with a friend because you're both feeling horny? What about sex you pay for from a sex worker who has unique skills and services? Or sex with an asexual partner who only wants to have sex once a year? These are all well documented human experiences, but naming them or actively seeking them can make people uncomfortable.

I've seen countless sitcoms pose the question: Can men and women be friends? The implication is people who have sexual attraction to each other cannot also be friends. Especially in a cis hetero paradigm, the assumption is that a man experiencing sexual attraction to a woman means that he is objectifying and dehumanizing her. If a woman is a friend, she is a whole human being, but if she suddenly becomes a sexual partner, she is an object of desire and no longer fully human.

When we take a step back to examine these narratives, we see a unique culture staring back at us. In the US especially, but in most white dominant cultures, there is a purposeful myth that white cultures are inherent or innate and everything else is weird. When we decentralize white American narratives we reveal the true diversity of human experiences. I'm reminded of learning about the Mosuo people, a small ethnic group that resides in the Yunnan and Sichuan provinces of China:

> Ethnographically, the Mosuo is probably most famous for its unique marriage pattern, the walking marriage where either woman or man will marry the other freely. The lovers meet at woman's house at night and the man returns to his own maternal family at dawn (Mathieu, 2000; Walsh, 2005), making it one of the very few societies where neither the males

nor the females disperse after marriage (known as duolocal residence; Ji et al., 2013). (Erping et al. 2022, p.5)

When young women come of age, they are given their own room with a separate entrance. They can give the key to their door to anyone they want and invite that person to their room to do whatever they want. In this community, a woman's brother takes on the role of helping parent and raises their sister's children, as the other bio parent is often unknown to everyone. The Mosuo are one of countless examples of communities whose approach to sexuality and relationships destabilizes the white western belief that sex, romance, marriage, and parenting have one correct configuration (romantic, long-term, heterosexual monogamy). In Western Africa it's common for Muslim families to include multiple wives in the practice of polygamy. There is a long history of women finding value and support in polygamous marriages—while these are as varied as the humans who create them, it's not uncommon for polygamy to provide status, companionship with other wives, opportunities for remarriage, and material stability (Lardoux and Van de Walle 2003). In the essay "Native American men-women, lesbians, two-spirits: Contemporary and historical perspectives," Sabine Lang writes that "ever since the beginning of European colonization of the Americas, there have been reports of male-bodied individuals in indigenous cultures taking up the work tasks of women, often also entering into relationships with men" (Lang 2016, p.299). She goes on to explore the complex nuances of sex, gender, and relationships in many North American cultures.

In many ways, this book is an ode to all the other configurations of sex, romance, marriage, parenting, love, and friendship. There are countless ways to build a human life. A relationship anarchist approach to life centers our humanity and invites the reality of our lived experience. Many of us are taught that sex dirties and dehumanizes our bodies, but we can see from investigation into ourselves and communities that already exist that it doesn't have to be that way. Sex can strengthen community bonds. Sex can build intimacy between friends. Sex can help us create new life. Sex can connect us to our innate birthright of pleasure.

THE IMPACT OF WESTERN CULTURAL NORMS

Humans have spent generations attempting to understand why societies form in the way they do, with their unique expectations, roles, and belief systems. It may seem obvious to some of us that certain ways of being are considered more normal, appropriate, and valid in our society than others. For example, heterosexuality, monogamy, marriage, and long-term partnership are all normalized, encouraged, and expected in the dominant Western white-supremacist culture. These expectations are imbued into the fabric of our lives from the time we are conceived. As we grow, the specific expectations shift, but the pervasive sense that there is a "right" or "wrong" way to do relationships permeates our bodies, psyches, and connections with others. We might find ourselves on a steady, linear trajectory of relationships like stepping onto an escalator and passively riding it up to the top, with no escape routes or detours, and only the option to go up.

The term "relationship escalator" was coined by Amy Gahran in a 2012 blog post shared on her site Solo Poly. This idea has become a valuable framework for understanding the norms, social pressures, and expectations of our society as we grow into adults. The relationship escalator describes the expectations placed on all of us to engage with our romantic relationships in a linear and hierarchical process. This process is taught to us in small and big ways, from explicit encouragement to get married and have children to the pervasive lack of representations of non-normative relationships in books and movies, and on television and social media.

Most of us are plopped on the bottom of the escalator when we're born, and it makes a steady upward trajectory from there. The escalator is very specific and predetermined. It tells us to be born to a cis straight mom and a cis straight dad. The doctors look at your genitals to determine your gender. Innies are girls, outies are boys. If the doctors can't tell if you're an inny or outy, they'll choose one for you. From infancy to puberty, you only have friends or family. Your life is purely platonic, with no sexual experiences. Romance can come in socially accepted packages like school dances or valentine's day. It's always straight. As a teen you can go on some dates and get your first kiss, maybe even have sex. Don't expect sex to feel too good if you're a girl. If you're a boy, be sure to have as much sex as possible. At 18 it's time to start looking for a serious partner. Once you find someone, you should date them for a year or two. Then, move in with them. Once you share a bed, get ready to combine all your belongings. This person should be everything to you, the most important relationship in your life. You should marry them. Have a big wedding with a white dress, suits, and color-coordinated outfits. Once you're married, get started on life. Buy a house and have a baby. Have another baby if you can. Don't fall in love with anyone else. Have sex regularly.

Stay in love. Stay together forever. Die in each other's arms. Okay, that's it!

While you read this example of the relationship escalator, I invite you to notice which parts have been true for you and which don't apply. Where did you deviate? Is this how you would describe the relationship escalator? You can write your own version! What am I missing, and what did I get right?

Many of us develop an intuitive awareness of the relationship escalator, even if we're not able to exactly place where or how we learned about these social expectations. Even those of us who have not developed this awareness, because of neurodivergence or because of growing up in a different culture, can sense that there is a set of rules.

As we explore relationships in this book, we can think about the kinds of relationships that are most meaningful to us. To begin this exploration, let's consider some questions about the relationship escalator and socio-cultural norms that we've just discussed. My hope is that these questions start to deepen your thinking about how you developed the view of the relationships that you have today. We can start a journey of exploration with curiosity. As you read this list, notice how these questions make you feel. Do they seem obvious, profound, or unhelpful? Do you notice openness, excitement, or resistance in your body?

Questions to ask yourself about the relationship escalator

- What messages did I get growing up about marriage and relationships?
- How do I feel about marriage? If marriage wasn't an option, what would I want instead?

- What was my relationship to sexuality as a child? As a teen? As a young adult? What is my relationship to sexuality now? What do I imagine for the future of my sexuality?
- Is it important that a romantic partner is the most important person in my life? What would I do if having a romantic partner wasn't an option?

Is there a "right" amount of sex to have in a marriage or romantic relationship? What would I do if this "right" amount wasn't an option for me? So how do we receive these messages? As children, we are deeply attuned to the ways our caregivers respond to our behaviors. If a caregiver gets angry, sad, or withdrawn because of something we do, we learn to expect and plan for this response. These patterns of learning are necessary for survival as children. We take in all the information around us like a sponge, receiving messages through body language and direct communication about how the world works. As a three-year-old my older brother was obsessed with the color pink. He wore exclusively pink for several years. As he approached kindergarten my mom started to become anxious that he would still want to wear pink at school. She was worried he would be bullied. In wanting to protect her child from harm she was faced with a challenging decision: How would she engage with her child's desire to wear pink? She decided to take a "neutral" approach by not commenting on his pink clothes positively or negatively. My brother did end up veering away from pink, although I'm not sure any of us know exactly why. I wonder what would have happened if my mom had made a concerted effort to celebrate and support my brother's choice to wear pink. Perhaps my brother would have felt affirmed at home, but less accepted at school due to bullying. Maybe he would have grown out of pink on his own, or maybe he would be wearing exclusively pink today! We'll never know. However, by doing nothing, my mom implicitly agreed not to challenge social norms that boys shouldn't wear pink. Without another script to follow, it's not surprising that my brother tended towards red, black, and green as he got older, all colors that are considered acceptable for boys.

We don't know exactly why or how my brother made sense of the world as a three-year-old choosing his favorite colors.[1] But we can identify the prevailing narrative about how children raised as boys are supposed to behave. I invite you to continue to bring your attention to these narratives and stories. As you do so, you may want to notice what comes up internally. Have you found yourself in alignment with social norms throughout your life? In which ways? Have you found yourself misaligned with social norms? How so? Which social norms bring you comfort? Which ones make you feel less safe?

If we decide we'd like to change social norms that aren't serving us or our communities, we might start by identifying exactly what is not working. But we can't stop there. In order to create change we have to replace the original script with something new. When I came out to my mom as bisexual, she responded with a blank affect and shrugged her shoulders. "I think I already knew that," was all she said. I felt a heaviness pull my body down like being covered in a blanket. I experienced this response as a rejection. I had been anxiously trying to find a time to share my experience with my mom, and it most certainly did not feel neutral or like a "small deal." Her intent

---

1   When I asked my brother about this he said that while he appreciated that my mom was trying to protect him from bullying, he also acknowledged that his life might have been very different if his love of pink had been celebrated and accepted.

was to normalize bisexuality by responding with neutrality and not "making a big deal out of it." The message I got was my mom didn't want to talk to me about my queerness. Even though my mom has been openly supportive of queer people my entire life, I went into the conversation with my mom expecting judgment and disapproval for being queer. I wanted her to show me enthusiastically how celebrated I am for being queer. Without something to hold on to, I immediately slipped back into the dominant paradigm. This is the epitome of how social norms function. Social norms are stories, narratives, perceptions, and judgments that seep into our interpersonal relationships even when we make an effort to dispel them.

The pastel pinks and blues of the movie But I'm a Cheerleader (2000) come to mind as I think about the relationship escalator. When I write it out in such blunt terms, it does seem especially absurd. We can see how while this is the norm and the social expectation, very few people fit into this script. Many of us become aware at a young age that there are expectations beyond our control. As children, there are so many things in our lives we don't get to control that it can be difficult to identify who we are and what we want. And yet, children regularly let us know when the adults around them are attempting to restrict their authentic expression. I find it magical to meet kids who have strong opinions about how they'd like to live their lives. Whether they are excited to wear a spiderman costume every day for a year or reject gender norms, children are incredible teachers when it comes to authenticity.

Once when my friend Charlie was seven (they are currently nine), they asked me what it meant to be bisexual. I told them it's when people like people who are a similar gender to them or a very different gender to them. They looked at me with a blank face and then said "well, duh," and went back to playing. The concept of liking people of multiple genders was so obvious to Charlie that having a specific word for it seemed asinine. I was (and am) truly obsessed with Charlie's worldview. It reminded me of how simple it could be to love people without judgment—in Charlie's world, bisexuality is an obvious way to relate. At the same time, Charlie once explained to me that our dogs had to get married because their dog is a girl and my dog is a boy and they are friends—in that moment, the psychic impact of the relationship escalator was at work. While younger generations are valuable models for self-acceptance and relational exploration, we still must continue to combat deeply ingrained stories about gender, relationships, and self-expression. These transformations start on an interpersonal level. As more kids grow up in a world where people are openly queer, trans, polyamorous, sex positive, and anti-racist, the more kids will grow up being able to choose intentionally the life they want to create.

Let me be clear. There is nothing wrong with getting married, having kids, and dying in your partner's arms. In fact, if that's what is working for you then it is truly beautiful. The core question is: Did you get to intentionally choose your life, or did you feel obligated to follow a certain path?

And if you did feel obligated to follow a certain path, how did you go about exiling or suppressing the parts of you that didn't want to conform? What do you do if you want to explore sexuality from a young age? What if you're a girl who wants to kiss girls or a boy who wants to kiss boys? What if you're not a girl or boy at all? What if you don't feel romantic love or sexual attraction? What if you don't want to get married? What if you have no desire to be a parent? What if your family and culture don't subscribe to these cis-hetero and white supremacist expectations? What if you love many people at once? What if you fall out of love with your partner? What if you prefer to make your choices on your own rather than with a partner? What if you like having a lot of sex every day? What if you're poor and you can't afford a house? What if you must take care of a sick family member? What if you're disabled and marriage means you will lose your government benefits?

If you felt yourself in any of these questions, you're in the right place. Relationship anarchy is a process of learning to live at odds with the system, but the reward is a return to our expansive, authentic selves.

LIVING AT ODDS WITH THE SYSTEM

There are countless ways that humans can't or don't want to fit into the relationship escalator. The relationship escalator is a systemic force that encourages conformity and suppresses authentic human expression, even for those who would freely choose that path. Many of us buy into this system because it's a lot easier than pushing back against it. It's extremely difficult to create a different path. However, it is possible. Some of us never get married, some of us get married lots of times. Some of us have pleasurable and consensual sexual experiences from a young age, some of us choose not to ever have sex. Some of us never have children, some of us help raise the children in our community as aunts, uncles, guncles, sparkles, and more.

When I interviewed my friend Mags (they/them), they spoke to the constraints that society exerted on their relational life. It took being in an environment saturated with queer, polyamorous people for Mags to learn about another option beyond monogamy. They explained that before moving to the Bay Area in California, they had only been exposed to non-monogamy in the form of polygamy practiced by some Mormon people. They shared the memory of watching the reality TV show *Sister Wives*, a TLC program that aired in 2010 and is still running.

That's all I knew about [non-monogamy] until I got to the Bay area, which was about three years ago. Everyone around here was just like, I'm poly, I'm poly. I do kitchen table,[2] I do non-hierarchical, I'm not monogamous and I was like, "What the, the fuck is all of this?" So, I was really, really confused. But the more that I spoke to people around me and especially my now partner...we started talking and they were a huge introduction to polyamory. They already were seeing a few people and consider some of their friends to be partners in just different ways. And I was just like, "How is this working? How is that happening?" So just like asking them a lot of questions like, "What do you do when you're feeling this way?" or like, "How do you deal with jealousy?" or like, "How do you give time or prioritize people?" Just asking them questions and figuring out how they dealt with it, it started to kind of make sense to why my past relationships weren't working for me.

Especially being that I never felt like one person could give me everything that I needed and I don't think that's a thing. But, realizing that and being like, "Oh, shit. Oh, I think I'm poly too!" Which I freaked out about a little bit too because I

---

2   Kitchen table polyamory describes an approach in which all (or most of) the partners in a polycule would be comfortable enough sitting at the kitchen table together. It does not necessarily mean everyone is close, although that could be the case, but that they can co-exist peacefully.

was just so used to being a monogamous [person] and that's how society taught me to be, especially in the Latino culture. You have one partner and it's usually a man and your world revolves around them. We were conditioned as women in a Latina household that your job was to learn how to cater to a man. And that's it. So, learning polyamory, it was just like, "oh, wait, like, I can play whatever role I want in any relationship." So that was like a big thing and, yeah, that's how I kind of got here.

Mags's experience illustrates the way our communities impact our perspective on what is "normal" and "appropriate." We look to the people around us to help us make sense of our experiences. If we find ourselves around a community of people who don't understand or choose not to understand our unique human experience, it can lead to extreme distress. If you find yourself in an environment of people who don't get you, you may find that it takes a toll on your well-being. It is well documented anecdotally and scientifically that being "othered," ostracized, or shunned by other humans is extremely detrimental. People who experience marginalization are acutely aware of the toll it takes on our brains to be constantly perceived as less human, less important, less capable, or less deserving of basic human rights than others. Knowing this, it can be challenging to opt into situations in which we know we'll be different.

Jibril (he/they) shared his experience of realizing the unique intersections between their Black experience and his queer experience. This realization "popped up to me," he explained:

I am a Black male-presenting young adult. Why in the world

would I ever choose to also add this, this, and this [queerness, gender expansiveness, and non-monogamy] onto the platter that is my existence? Knowing how the world treats it. Now in my life having gone through it... I don't wanna change anything about that. Like, I only wanna better myself. But I can imagine for so many people if they weren't given the choice, right? If there was a moment where you sit down and know how the world is and they give you the choice, do you want to be like this or do you want to conform to everyone else? Most people would probably at that moment, out of fear, out of self-preservation, choose to go with the thing that makes them as normal as possible.

Jibril shares with us the complexity of navigating multiple marginalized experiences. They state that even though he wouldn't give up their experience of exploring queerness and experiencing a deeper self-actualization, he sees how challenging this path is. More, Jibril reminds us that as humans we are all seeking to survive, but what is possible beyond just survival? Jibril may be right to assume that some people would choose an easier, less complicated path if given the option. And yet, so many of us do choose a more painful path because there is something undeniably seductive about exploration, self-expression, and resistance. Still, many folks find that relationship anarchy is not accessible to them because it does require so much time and energy, and it is deeply counter-cultural. For folks who are existing in survival mode, simply trying to live in a world that is actively attempting to kill them, adding another layer of "otherness" to one's identity may not be possible.

At the same time, many marginalized folks find that

non-normative practices like relationship anarchy are essential to their survival in this hostile world. Creating networks of care beyond romantic relationships can help folks sustain life in creative and unique ways. Imagine how helpful it would be to have multiple loving adults in a kid's life who can quickly and effectively help with childcare when needed. Or, what if you had a partner who has a very different racial and/or cultural experience from you? Might it be helpful to have someone else in your life who can cry or celebrate with you when your partner doesn't get it? What would it be like to know that living in a multi-generational household was normalized and respected (as it is in so many cultures)? Relationship anarchy is simply a framework through which to explore human connection in a way that makes authentic sense to us.

The takeaway here is not that some relationship styles (monogamy, marriage, heterosexuality) are inherently bad and that others (polyamory, queerness) are good. That would just be doing the relationship escalator with a different set of expectations! We all deserve the opportunity to explore what combination of these relationship styles feels best to us. Sydney Rae Chin (they/them), a queer sex educator, exemplified this when discussing their marriage.

As a married person right now, even if my marriage were to de-escalate or to form into something else, I can imagine myself still being in a platonic marriage. Like, it doesn't need to be sexual if that just isn't what works for us at some point after having a kid or whatever.' Cause he's my husband; my husband is one of my best friends. Yeah, the sex is a nice bonus, not gonna lie. Sex is always a nice bonus. But also, it's not necessary 'cause a relationship is more than sex and it's more than love.

Sydney describes their marriage as something mutable, alive, and nuanced. They can hold that while sex in their relationship is enjoyable now, it may not always be desired by one or any partners in the relationship. Without rejecting marriage as a valid form of connection or creating an unrealistic standard of how a marriage must be, Sydney (and their husband) are co-creating a relationship that works uniquely for them. A foundational tenet of relationship anarchy is this unique co-creation. Relationship anarchy reminds us that we are primarily relating to other humans, not other relational concepts. This calls to mind something my partner Zee says to me: "There's no secret greater force in this relationship, it's just us figuring this out together."

And yet, there are also systemic forces at work shaping and influencing our choices. When we open ourselves up to the idea that we don't have to do what we've been taught to do, we also open ourselves up to a deluge of uncertainty and potential judgment. My intention here is not to shame those of us who align with dominant paradigms, but to invite us into more nuance. Can we hold that marriage has historically been a tool of white supremacy to control and subdue marginalized people *and* that it is a valid way to create community, share resources, and establish trust between partners? I think we can! Anarchist values invite us into this nuance. Rather than espousing a unique agenda, anarchists encourage us to critique the agendas we ourselves create. Thus, we can never be too certain we've arrived at a place more ethical, radical, or profound than any other. Our work is to feel into how things are going for everyone and change them up when we see someone is suffering.

Niki (they/them), a neuroqueer[3] parent, illustrated the way political and social engagement is intertwined with relationships. "I'm very left radical," they explained:

> I think that's relevant. Because that's also about, who do I want to connect with? More than people being of any genders, it's really like, can I flow with them politically? That's really a big part of my being in the world. I don't believe that anybody has the perfect analysis politically at all. That's not it, I don't want to come across as though I know it all or anything. Everybody has so much to learn, but I can't get really close to anyone who's not interested in things being okay for everybody. Like, sorry, put it right.

Niki is describing an approach to relationships that does not divorce politics from love. They remind us that while navigating a world full of systemic oppression, violence, and unequal power dynamics, it's valuable to be able to acknowledge and deconstruct these forces in our relationships. Niki implicitly speaks to the way their identity as queer and trans is inherently related to their political community. More important than gender, to Niki, is alignment in the belief that all humans

---

3 The verb "to neuroqueer" was initially developed by Nick Walker, Athena Lynn Michaels-Dillon, and Remi Yergeau to describe the process of engaging in, expressing, shaping, developing something in relation to neurodivergence and queerness: "A neuroqueer individual is any individual whose identity, selfhood, gender performance, and/or neurocognitive style have in some way been shaped by their engagement in practices of neuroqueering, *regardless of what gender, sexual orientation, or style of neurocognitive functioning they may have been born with*." (neuroqueer.com)

deserve to be okay and that when things are not working for some of us, we should endeavor to make it right. Niki's perspective calls to mind adrienne maree brown's assertion that social change begins at the minute, interpersonal level. In her book *Pleasure Activism: The Politics of Feeling Good* she writes:

> We need radical honesty—learning to speak from our root systems about how we feel and what we want. Speak our needs and listen to others' needs. To say, "I need to hear that you miss me." "When you're high all the time it's hard for me to feel your presence." "I lied." "The way you talked to that man made me feel unseen." "Your jealousy makes me feel like an object and not a partner." The result of this kind of speech is that our lives begin to align with our longings, and our lives become a building block for authentic community and ultimately a society that is built around true need and real people, not fake news and bullshit norms. (2019, p.19)

Relational intimacy and social change are intertwined. Compatibility, intimacy, and radical honesty create the building blocks of a community in which people matter. When we prioritize partners who are in alignment with this project of social care, we intertwine our commitment to social justice in the fabric of our relational lives.

Yael (she/her/ella), a sex, intimacy, identity, and relationship coach, also spoke to the importance of being in alignment, often through shared experiences and/or values, with the relationships she chooses. She explained to me that for her:

> there is safety in the things that do not need to be spoken. And it doesn't mean I won't speak it, I'm verbose and I overexplain, but I breathe more freely when someone else

just gets it. The feeling of not having to translate—they just know because they, too, have lived it. More recently, I've been attracting a lot of neurodivergent folks into my life as I've been unmasking. We connect through our neuro spici-ness—understanding each other with no need for apology for atypical tendencies...and the fact that things don't look the same way and how that interacts with our understanding of anti-racism and the work that we're doing towards that. So, what does it look like in our communities to work to be pro-trans, Black, Indigenous? There is no pulling apart of politics in life. I just said to a friend yesterday, "I can't have people in my life with whom I can't discuss politics and therefore I cannot have people in my life who do not have the same politics because it's not an option just to talk about other things. I don't know what else to talk about."

Yael is speaking to her experience of affinity, alignment, or compatibility. For her, pro-trans, pro-Black, pro-Indigenous politics are such an integral part of the way she moves through the world, that relating to someone on a deep, intimate level who doesn't share these values would be unsustainable. What are your political values? How do they show up in your relationships?

FINDING AFFINITY

While interviewing Mora (they/them), they emphasized the importance of identifying the ways we are in affinity with one another, in other words, the way we discover our alliances, commonalities, and shared values. They reminded me of a shift I've seen many non-monogamous folks go through as they explore relationships. When first exploring non-monogamy it is not uncommon to connect with any and all people you feel interested in. The rush of freedom that comes with exploring non-monogamy can be a little overwhelming. I've watched countless friends and lovers embark on relational journeys that ended up being incompatible for them down the line. I've done my own share of jumping into dynamics that I knew were maybe not the best fit for me! It's easy to prioritize chemistry over compatibility.

What does it look like to hold space for both chemistry and compatibility without swinging too far in either direction? How do we affirm our body's desire for certain humans while identifying who is truly in alignment with our values? How do we discover ourselves through deepening intimacy with another person?

In relationship anarchy we get to create unique relationships with anyone we want in any way we want. So, in a situation where we might have broken up with or stopped talking to someone in a monogamous framework, in a relationship anarchy framework we can develop a relationship with them that feels right to us, even if that means only seeing each other once a year, or only talking about our hobbies. In this way we can merge compatibility with chemistry; we don't have to choose one or the other. We can honor our desire by creating a relationship that is actually compatible with our lives. Relationship anarchy invites us to critically think about who we want in our life, how we want to show up for these people, and how we want our people to show up for us. We are invited into a deeper responsibility for ourselves and our communities.

This model of relationships supports the reality that we all have different capacities for connection and for life-building. We may feel a deep love and appreciation for someone, but not have the compatibility required to live together, share resources, or support each other emotionally. That doesn't mean that our relationship doesn't matter. This philosophy extends to folks in our communities who have immense value as humans (as all humans do) but don't conform to capitalist or white supremacist expectations of how humans should function. In relationship anarchy we prioritize people. For those of us with physical or mental disabilities, this kind of reframing can be liberating. Rather than being punished because we can't conform to society's expectations, we can build relationships outside of these expectations that are supportive to us and our capacities. What if we could show up to relationships with our neurodivergence and disability and trust that our partners would let us know what they can hold and how? What if we could rely on a complex system of humans to support our needs rather than just family or just partners?

Many queer people will already be familiar with the idea of creating supportive care systems through chosen family. Scientific studies have begun to reinforce knowledge that the queer community has known experientially for years: Queerness is inherently intertwined with other counter-cultural traits like neurodivergence, disability, Blackness, Indigeneity, and sexual diversity. These counter-cultural ways of being require us to develop community outside of the norms. In an interview with Nick Walker, a neurodivergent, queer and trans theorist who began developing the verb "to neuroqueer" in 2008, I asked her if there is a connection between being queer, neurodivergent, and resisting oppressive social norms. She responded, "Yes, being a member of any group that's marginalized and oppressed by prevailing social norms and systems is probably the number one way for people to get started on the path of thinking critically about those norms and systems. It's certainly what got me started in that direction!"

In 2022 Almah LaVon Rice wrote an incredible piece on the blog We Create Space titled "The Art of Black, Queer, Neurodivergent Survival." LaVon Rice offers a portal of self-devotion through mixed media art forms. Not only is this article beautifully written poetry, but it is full of poignant and expansive reflections on the interplay between queerness, neurodivergence, Blackness, womanhood, and the threads that intertwine these experiences. LaVon Rice (2022) writes, "Black neuroqueer womanhood is not a curse but a whole universe— and the indeterminacy and expansiveness of abstract art point to how I am various, irreducible, and free. In a society dead-set on putting me in its demographic cages, art gives me a way to slip through the bars, if only for a moment."

These words remind me of another wise soul, Nazeil (he/they), a self-described "white, trans, gender fluid, queer, Jewish, polyamorous, slutty, kinky, autistic, triple taurus." They shared with me that self-actualization, sex, and pleasure are all special interests[4] in their neurodivergent landscape. Their neurodivergence has been a pathway to deeper connection, intimacy, and liberatory connections. Atira, a queer, nonbinary, Black femme, and self-described "silly goose," also told me that human relationships and connection are some of their special interests. When talking about exploring relationships, Atira noted how deeply fascinating they find it to discuss the nuances of connection with potential or current partners. Atira and Nazeil, in sharing their neurodivergent joy for human connection, model how playful and enjoyable

---

4   A special interest is a specific topic, often niche, that an autistic and/or neurodivergent person becomes profoundly knowledgeable about and/or engaged in.

relationship anarchy can be. Neurodivergence can be a pathway to pleasure. Non-normative brains, bodies, and desires are portals through which we can meet and remeet our authentic human desires.

Of course, relationship anarchy is full of hard work and boring, mundane moments, but it is uniquely defined by the commitment relationship anarchists hold to authentic expression of self. More specifically, an authentic expression of self that can intermingle and collaborate with the authentic expressions of others. At its core, relationship anarchy is a practice of play and creation. We commit ourselves to building and rebuilding connections in the same way that we take apart and put together Legos, puzzles, or clay. Our shared goal is not productivity, purity, or the agglomeration of wealth, but the pursuit of pleasure, embodiment, and authentic connection.

So how do we find the space in which play is possible? How do we build enough safety and security to feel comfortable exploring our inner worlds? What is the interplay between our own pursuit of pleasure and that of others? How do we negotiate our self-expression when it is activating or uncomfortable for the people we love? How do we honor our needs without denying or rejecting the needs of others? From these questions we will dive into the practical, day-to-day construction of relationship anarchy.

CHAPTER 3

The Foundations of Relations

Relationship Anarchy is the practice of trying to take away all of the stories that are being told about the people and the relationship and focus on the needs, feelings, and boundaries of the people involved in the relationship.

ZEE, AN INTERVIEWEE

CARING FOR EACH OTHER

When people hear the term "anarchy," they get understandably stressed. Anarchy is associated with chaos, violence, and discord. How do we create relationships that are supportive for us? There may be some chaos and some discord, but we all deserve safety. And yet, safety is a tricky concept. In the book *Trauma Stewardship* (2009), Laura Van Dernoot Lipsky explores this reality with compassion and care. Her approach to tending to others with care and longevity, what she calls trauma stewardship, includes living with the realities that we are always at risk of injury, loss, and death. We cannot guarantee life or trust between ourselves and others, no matter how deeply we crave it. And humans do crave it. We crave safety so intensely that sometimes we will do the exact opposite of what we really need in order to feel safe.

I once had a friend who seemed to constantly be drawn to romantic partners who were the exact opposite of what she said she wanted. It was difficult to watch my friend reject kind-hearted souls for people who lied to her and broke their promises, and over time I noticed my empathy waning for her experience. Her choices reminded me of the people I used to date and had been actively working so hard to avoid. When she made the choices I tried so hard to avoid, it reminded me how much energy I was exerting to be "healed." Part of me still believed that I didn't really deserve safety, and dating someone who was clearly emotionally unavailable was actually easier than dating someone who really saw me, because vulnerability felt unsafe. Unpacking those habits and changing my behavior was hard, grueling work. Part of me was resentful of my friend who, in my mind, didn't have to do the hard work!

With some reflection, I was able to see how I was projecting my own feelings onto my friend's experience. My friend was on her own journey, and my lack of empathy for her actually came from my lack of empathy for myself. Witnessing my friend reminded me of the ways I judge myself for not being "healed enough," or for making mistakes.

Even when our behaviors seem self-sabotaging, they are usually coming from a place of yearning for an unmet need, which is always deserving of empathy. For example, dating an emotionally unavailable person can provide familiarity, clarity, and a sense of certainty: I know how this person will act; it may not be good, but at least I don't have to hope they will be kind and then be disappointed.

So how do we care for ourselves when sometimes we crave the exact things that hurt us? It takes an immense amount of time and energy to understand our habits and challenge the ways we move through the world. If you are reading this book because you're interested in changing the way you relate to other humans, you're probably going to come up against some deep internal wounds. Relationship anarchy is a beautiful, expansive, and radical way to engage with those around us, and it can also be triggering. Seeing a partner hold hands with their lover, watching a friendship bloom into a partnership, realizing that a romantic love is no longer romantic, expressing desire for intimacy and being met with disinterest: These are just a few examples of how relating to others can be scary. There are countless ways we can be hurt by others, and that's true in all relationships. But, in relationship anarchy we open ourselves up to more fluidity, and with that comes more uncertainty. Monogamy can offer us a satisfying promise of safety: I will love only you. If we keep something locked down, just for us, maybe it can't be touched by the uncertainties of life! Right?

Well, maybe! Just like everything, there is no 100 percent right path forward that fits everyone's needs. I often say to clients, I'm less interested in exactly what structure your relationship is than what it feels like to be in that relationship structure.

- Do you feel like you get to be your full self, showing up with vulnerability, intimacy, and connection?
- Do you feel safe enough to share your boundaries and needs?

- Do you feel safe enough to bring up messy feelings like anger, fear, and sadness?
- Do you feel supported day to day to get your work done, care for the humans who need care, and have time for yourself?

It is possible to feel an enthusiastic yes to all these things, no matter the relationship style. It's also possible to offer a nuanced *sort of* and still feel good about your relationship style. You might also say fuck yes to some of these questions and fuck no to others. Maybe that's a sign to bring more attention to certain parts of your relationship. What do you need to revise, question, or challenge to get your needs met?

EMBRACING YOUR INNATE ANARCHIST

One of my favorite ways to bring up relationship anarchy to monogamous couples is to ask them about their wedding. These days most people pick and choose their favorite parts of wedding ceremonies from innumerable cultural heritages. I like to ask couples which parts of their wedding they chose, and which parts they felt forced into. If they could go back and do it again, what would they do differently? Not only do I think it's cute and profound to discuss marriage ceremonies, but it's also a helpful window into the mindset of a monogamous couple. How many requirements were there at the wedding? Was it a joyous day or full of stress? Did you write your own vows? What did your vows say? Did you discuss with a religious leader or counselor what the agreements or expectations of the marriage would be? How did you feel leading up to the wedding day? Did you like what you were wearing? Did you feel like yourself?

A wedding ceremony can sometimes be a microcosm of a couple's experience of each other and the world around them. If a couple isn't married it's also insightful to ask them why and how they made that choice. Looking back on a wedding ceremony provides three things. One, it provides insight on how invested all the participants felt in the dominant cultural paradigm at the time. Two, it gives important information about what is important to this pair. And three, it begins the conversation about building relationships based on needs versus norms.

Let's talk about this idea of needs versus norms. Norms are social and cultural expectations predetermined about our lives without our consent. They are usually formed over time from many different cultural authorities, such as the church, government, elders, parents, and systems of bureaucracy. Needs are innate human requirements that we must tend to in order to survive and/or thrive. When we build relationships based on norms, we attempt to meet our needs through the insight and expectations of those who have shaped dominant paradigms, rather than our unique, complex selves. We do things like proclaim that trans people shouldn't be able to get life-affirming surgery because historically trans people haven't been able to get life-affirming surgery. We expect marriages to last for a whole lifetime. We punish humans for seeking sex outside of marriage. We ridicule people who want community but not children. We berate beings who don't experience sexual or romantic attraction, and we attempt to convert those who love beyond heterosexual paradigms.

When we center needs over norms, we look carefully at the individual and the collective. We consider what humans need to survive and thrive to be inextricable. We value weird art, new words, unique expressions, rest, and neurodivergence. We also value such things as communal responsibility, mutual aid, co-parenting, shared homes, gardens, community fridges, access to healthcare and housing, and widespread accessibility. When we prioritize needs, we're able to utilize norms as tools rather than as laws. An example: We could create a norm that people are expected to offer some amount of their salary to the collective to support human services (AKA taxes)! This norm functions well until suddenly the majority of our community loses their employment because they all come down with a strange flu. Suddenly this norm doesn't function as well as we want it to. Okay, we say, let's re-evaluate. These unemployed folks shouldn't owe what they don't have, right? Let's brainstorm how our unemployed folks and our employed folks can help each other. We can identify the resources we do have and allot them where they are needed, and then consider a new system of taxes that will effectively serve everyone.

In my interviews, I noticed that countless people identified a tension between their beliefs and practices. I was struck by the way Nazeil described his experience of relationship anarchy as an autistic person. "Being autistic, change is really really hard," they explained. And yet, in his relationship with their partner Ethan, change is a constant. In their relationship, friendships are fluid and anything could happen when hanging with a friend, including sexual or romantic explorations.

Nazeil explained the process he went through learning to surrender to this change, how he navigated waves of acceptance and resistance. He and his partner Ethan (he/they) described many different tools they use to work with their neurodivergences, trauma responses, and unique anxieties. They both expressed an appreciation for the personal growth that practicing relationship anarchy has offered them, even though it has been dysregulating much of the time. They shared a foundational belief that the relationship they were forming was important and aligned with their values. This shared belief helped guide and soothe the moments of dysregulation. Still, it can be very disorienting to align with a certain set of beliefs and find that your body is not as enthusiastic as your brain. Asho Alvarez (they/them) emphasized this when I asked them what they wished they'd known before starting their relationship anarchy journey. "It's okay for it to be messy," they explained, "it's okay to notice that you still have heteronormative ideas."

I am inspired by this idea of messiness, of noticing the nuance and/or discrepancies between brain and body. Moss (they/them), a Black, poly non-binary, and trans parent, explained how the process of exploring our bodies and brains can be slow and complicated. When I asked them how they navigate relationships when they notice a discontinuity between brain and body they explained:

> I think it's a lot of trying to get back in my body and clock when I've left it and clock when my nervous system is like "this is scary!" So, it's slow and it's personal and it's not exciting. It's a lot of DBT[1] skill work. Like mindfulness. But I feel like we can't show up for this work unless we can be in our bodies, and that's a big conversation with queers or folks that are trans or on any of our intersection points.

Moss reminds us of how slow and challenging this work can be. Even in mostly secure relationships with great communication,

---

1   Dialectical behavioral therapy.

clarity, consent, and love, we will inevitably experience distress, hurt, and sadness. What is your tolerance for difficult emotions? Do you notice getting overwhelmed or shutting down when big feelings arise? Do you prefer to process feelings alone or with others?

Tracking the connection between our thoughts and our feelings calls to mind an early experience I had with polyamory. A partner of mine met someone on a dating app and shared with me how excited they were to go on a first date. Their excitement was infectious, and I found myself feeling a joyous compersion[2] for their upcoming date. I loved my partner, and it made so much sense to me that other people would love them too, so I didn't want to restrict anyone from experiencing their beauty. When the actual date rolled around, I found that I was jealous, scared, and dysregulated. I could hardly look my partner in the eyes. Disoriented that I was suddenly feeling so bad, I pretended that I was fine and tried to behave like my normal self. They left for their date, and I begrudgingly hugged them goodbye. Alone, I was sullen and grumpy all night. I couldn't fall asleep and I had no appetite. I couldn't stop wondering about the date. What was happening? Were they kissing? Having sex? Falling in love?

When my partner got back home from their date, my feelings were hard to hide. I didn't want to look at them or be in the same room. I knew it wasn't fair to take out my feelings on them, but I didn't know what else to do with my feelings! The feelings I was having felt wrong, and I just wanted them to go away. In response to my cold and unwelcoming behavior, my partner started to feel guilty and ashamed that they had

---

2   The emotion or experience of feeling joy and excitement when a partner connects with someone else.

a nice time. I took both of us on an emotional roller coaster. When my partner tried to disconnect and tend to their own needs, I lashed out angrily because I felt abandoned. When they tried to soothe or repair, I pushed them away because I felt I couldn't trust them. After about a day I was able to calm my nervous system and return to my partner with tentative openness. We discussed the experience, naming which parts felt hurtful and doing our best to listen without judgment. Looking back, I see so many more dynamics playing out than I did at the time.

First, I realized that I didn't feel as fully positive and joyful when I first heard about the date as I thought I did. I was so concerned with being perceived as "good" at polyamory that I suppressed my scary, messy feelings until they were out of control. Second, I didn't know how to hold the conflict between my thoughts and my feelings. Some of my thoughts were positive and hopeful, some were anxious and resentful. Some of my feelings were intense and painful, some were neutral, and some felt good. At the time, I didn't know how to hold all these things in my body at once. I still find it hard to this day!

Moss articulated this tension so beautifully: "You are a body, in a lot of ways. And that part of your experience I don't think can be discounted when you're playing and maybe something doesn't go right or maybe you said something wrong." Moss went on to give the example of watching friends play or make art in the same room as you while you're not included.

Maybe in theory you know that it's cool for these people to be making art right now and I'm not included, but as a nervous system, can it be okay that other people are playing without you and can you trust that they love you? You don't need to co-regulate with them. You can regulate on your own and just kind of like stay in that stream of play. Does that make sense?

It does make sense, Moss! We are called in relationship anarchy to identify our nervous system's capacity to navigate complex relational situations. Humans really like having the attention of other humans. Humans can get scared when the people they love aren't paying attention to them. And, humans are capable of building trust with other people. Humans can learn to soothe their own bodies when other humans aren't available. Humans can develop an immense capacity for nuance.

What if, not that many years ago, I had started listening to my partner telling me about their date with a full embrace of my messiness? What if I had given myself permission to be excited for my partner *and* upset they were leaving me home alone at the same time? What if I had trusted that I could feel joyful and abandoned all at once? This brings me to another important insight that came up again and again in my interviews. The idea that relationship anarchy opened and expanded people's understanding of attachment.

ATTACHMENT

Attachment is, at its core, a biological process of our human bodies that allows us to connect and bond to other humans in order to stay alive. It is a process that begins before we are even conceived, as it has already been operating for many generations before us. Attachment is the connection we have with our caregivers: the pervasive feeling that no matter how bad things get, the people who take care of us matter. It is first experienced with the adults who raise us because we are uniquely dependent on them to keep us alive.

While theories of attachment have blossomed into many things, it was the psychologist and psychiatrist John Bowlby who was first credited with his theory of attachment in infants with their caregivers (Bowlby 1958, 1988). Bowlby theorized that infants are wired to create connection with their caregivers, actively updating their behaviors based on their caregivers' responses to their bids for connection and soothing. Bowlby suggested that the emotional landscape of a parent or caregiver directly impacts the way a child develops their emotional landscape. Mary Ainsworth, another psychologist, and John Bowlby showed that children's attachment styles can be either more secure or more insecure, depending on how well a caregiver can attune to their child's needs and respond to their needs effectively (Bretherton 1992).

In the 1980s, psychologists Cindy Hazan and Phillip Shaver theorized that romantic love was its own attachment process. Hazan and Shaver drew the connection between attachment styles formed in childhood (secure, avoidant, anxious/ambivalent) and attachment dynamics playing out between adults in romantic partnerships (secure, avoidant, anxious, disorganized) (Hazan and Shaver 1987). While romantic adult partnerships are not undergirded by a dependence on someone else to survive, our bodies may experience them in this way. I have heard friends and clients say countless times: I don't know how I will survive if they (my partner) leave(s) me.

When I first learned about attachment, I was unsettled by the rigid definitions described. I remember reading a blog post that explained the four attachment styles in adults: secure, anxious/preoccupied, avoidant/dismissive, or disorganized/fearful-avoidant. I found it difficult to determine where in this schema I would place myself. All of the attachment styles described different parts of my emotional landscape, and every relationship I had activated a slightly different attachment relationship to myself and to others. I decided that the closest fit for me was anxiously attached, and I held that identity marker for a long time, consuming any information I could on anxious attachment and how to move towards secure attachment. While this is not everyone's experience, I became aware that I was ashamed and embarrassed by my anxious attachment, and that my journey to "heal" myself was in fact exacerbating my anxiously attached traits even further as I was unconsciously shaming myself for being "needy," which led me to feel more neediness and abandonment.

It wasn't until I read Jessica Fern's iconic book *Polysecure: Attachment, Trauma, and Consensual Nonmonogamy* (2020) that attachment as a concept took on a much more nuanced, and more helpful, framework in my brain and body. What I experienced in Fern's writing was a profound deepening of the concept of attachment from something that is innate in a person to something that is formed, reformed, and in flux between all beings. Fern shares with us the Nested Model of Attachment and Trauma, a multi-faceted and integrated model of attachment that includes our internal and external experiences of the world (see Figure 3.1). Fern moves beyond attachment as it pertains to self and relationships, and expands our view. "The levels of home, culture, society and the collective all factor into how safe and secure we feel in the world, with others and within ourselves... For example, consider poverty, gender expectations or institutionalized birth practices, and how each of these may impact attachment and trauma" (p.78).

Figure 3.1 Nested model of attachment and trauma

What Fern helps us understand is that all spectrums of attachment can emerge and exist within one person, one relationship, one community, one society, and one collective, and thus there are countless configurations of attachment present in our internal and external experiences. I highly recommend reading the first couple chapters of *Polysecure* to deepen your understanding of attachment and familiarize yourself with the nuances of these attachment styles. For now, let's review the basics of each attachment style, bearing in mind that the human expression of these styles is nuanced and complex.

Secure Attachment: Humans with secure attachment are mostly able to effectively move through moments of dysregulation and return to a secure, balanced internal state alone or with help from others. When conflict arises, securely attached humans have a larger window of tolerance for distress. They are likely to respond to conflict or tension with calm, compassion, or curiosity. Securely attached humans will find they can move from solo activities to connection with others without serious distress. They are likely to reach out for support and connection when they are having a hard time and when they're celebrating something good.

Anxious/Preoccupied Attachment: Humans with anxious attachment may find they are especially preoccupied with the reactions and responses of humans they feel connected to. They are likely to feel anxiety (such as heart beating, eyes scanning, tummy ache) when they notice a shift in the behavior of someone they are close to. In conflict, they will use whatever tools they have to maintain closeness and avoid losing the relationship. These tools, such as demanding communication, crying, yelling, trying to control others, or becoming angry may or may not be effective for this goal. Anxiously attached humans are likely to seek closeness and comfort when they are upset, and to protest if care is not available or consistent.

Avoidant/Dismissive Attachment: Humans with avoidant attachment may find that being alone, retreating, or staying numb are the safest-feeling options for them when it comes to human connection. This isn't because avoidantly attached humans don't crave connection; they do, but they may find that the risk of connection is so great that it's just not possible to come out of their safe shell. Avoidantly attached humans may push people away with body language or words if they feel someone is threatening their safe bubble. The more pressure an avoidantly attached person feels to come out of their shell, the deeper they may retreat. Many avoidantly attached humans can get overwhelmed by other people's feelings and their own, leading to shut down and freeze states in their nervous system.

Disorganized/Fearful Attachment: Humans with disorganized attachment are likely to feel a combination of anxious and avoidant attachment responses back and forth or at the same time. Disorganizedly attached humans are likely to feel an inner conflict and chaos when it comes to human connection. Their bodies, unsure how to navigate the experience of feeling constantly unsafe in relationships, will try any protective mechanisms available to keep them safe. This may look like retreating, shutting down, disconnecting and/or escalating conflict, obsessively reaching out, and/or demanding to not be left alone. Disorganized attachment is sometimes described as having one foot on the brake and one foot on the gas; it is a flooding of emotions and sensations in response to perceived threat.

- Which of these attachment styles do you see yourself in, if any?
- Does your experience of attachment change depending on the person you're with?
- What happens if you have conflict with multiple people who you relate to differently?
- Are there any protective behaviors (i.e. silence, seeking touch, taking time alone, or escalating conflict) that you use most regularly?

If you want to get vulnerable, have someone in your life read this section on attachment and ask them what they think your attachment style is. Has it changed since you first met? Does it change depending on the situation?

Check out this quiz from the book *Attached* by Amir Levine and Rachel Heller (2011) to learn more about you and your partner's attachment styles.[3]

---

3   www.attachedthebook.com/wordpress/compatibility-quiz

As Jessica Fern articulates, we are intertwined in the lives of other beings on all levels of existence, from the bacteria that help us break down the food in our gut to the star dust that formed the planet we live and change with. We are enmeshed in the feedback loops of existence, constantly receiving and offering to those around us, impacting the world in ways we may never understand. And, we are also intimately aware of the impacts we make when we feel the repercussions in our little bubble. Part of the relational work we are embarking on is taking responsibility for our impact, and in order to do that, we must first discuss power.

POWER DYNAMICS

In all relationships there are power dynamics. Power dynamics will impact our relationships whether we choose to acknowledge them or not. Power comes in many forms, and its forms change throughout history. What has brought someone power at one point in time may lead to marginalization or disenfranchisement at another time. Sometimes we see these shifts happening in real time, like when cis straight white men proclaim that they aren't allowed to say anything anymore! When actually, being a bully is no longer being tolerated or celebrated in the way it used to be (at least in some spaces). People with privilege sometimes experience the redistribution of power as a kind of marginalization for them. If you're used to getting more power and privilege than someone else, the redistribution of that power might feel really scary, because you're losing something. What people in privileged positions often forget is that we've already lost something: connection to our humanity. When we create and uphold violent power differentials, we deny and suppress the parts of us that yearn for authentic connection. In order to create equity, those with power will have to give up certain benefits, and that's okay. It will be scary, and uncertain, but the reward will be a reconnection to our deep human longing for love, community, and mutual support. What would you be willing to give up in order to bring more equity to the world?

I recently taught a class on Loving Conflict with my friend and colleague Alaina Knox (they/she). Alaina introduced me to the power wheel (Figure 3.2), a visual representation of some intersections of power in our current society.

Take a minute to look at this wheel of power. What comes up for you as you think about power and privilege? This is a visual that can begin a conversation, but it should not be the end of one. Something to note is that each of these identities is represented as being distinct from the others. We know from the theories of intersectionality offered by Kimberlé Crenshaw and other Black womanist scholars that none of these categories is truly distinct (Crenshaw 2017). A homeless neurotypical person does not have the same experience as a homeless neurodivergent person. Each identity marker added to someone's personhood complicates and influences all the other identities they hold. And each person will embody the complexities of their identity in a way that is unique to them.

It is also important to note that some of these identities are more stable than others, but even the ones we consider stable can shift in meaning depending on the context we inhabit. For example, I recently watched a clip of the popular reality TV show *America's Next Top Model*. It was a clip from one of the first seasons in which the show had a "plus size model." Among the other models you can tell this "plus size model" is larger, but she still looks very thin compared to an average person.

In the context of modeling, she experiences ridicule and judgment for the larger size of her body, but in the broader social context, she would benefit from the privilege of being thin. In fact, being thin enough to be considered worthy of modeling is a privilege in itself, but as the communities of privilege and power shift, so do the relational impacts of that privilege and power.

WHEEL OF POWER/PRIVILEGE

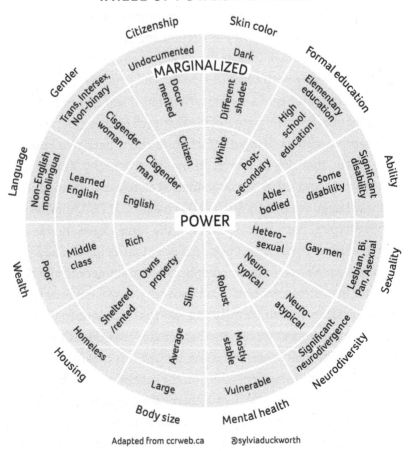

Figure 3.2 Wheel of power and privilege

There are some clear power differentials in the US that permeate most social and relational contexts, even if we aren't aware of them. Once we learn about power and privilege, it is our responsibility individually and collectively to understand and deconstruct the way power influences our relationships. This doesn't mean that power differentials are inherently bad or evil; in fact, it's possible to utilize our proximity to power in service of those we love who hold less power in certain contexts. For example, if you are a white person you might use your body at a protest to protect Black, Indigenous, or People of Color from the police, or if you're neurotypical you might help out a neurodivergent friend by body-doubling with them so they can get logistics tasks done. Remember, these examples are deeply contextual. It is also possible to reinforce power differentials by assuming certain people need or want your help when that's not actually the case.

Some people believe that ignoring power dynamics is an effective way to reduce their impact on people. I think of this approach as an "avoid the ghosts" mentality. It's like choosing to live in a haunted house, tip-toeing around trying not to piss off the ghosts. The thinking is, if we don't do anything the ghosts don't like, they'll leave us alone. (Did anyone else grow up in a household that also utilized this technique when it came to power, conflict, or intense emotions?) Living peacefully with ghosts is often possible for periods of time, or when everyone has a lot of energy to invest in not pissing off the ghosts. The problem here is that it's difficult to avoid ghosts forever when ghosts are temperamental and humans are messy. At some point someone is going to say or do the provocative something, and the ghosts are going to respond. Or we might find that someone living in the home gets tired of tiptoeing around and being quiet. Some of us like to be loud and messy, even if ghosts don't like it.

Another approach to navigating the power dynamics that imbue our world is to do a séance.[4] Instead of ignoring these inequalities, we can call them into existence. The thing about a séance is, it's inherently messy. Inviting the reality of power dynamics into the world with intention has consequences. If you haven't watched any scary movies with exorcisms recently I highly recommend it. Not only do horror films touch on the shadows of human existence that we are often so reluctant to explore (that's a separate book), they also remind us of our capacity for emotion. The day-to-day equivalents of ghosts and monsters are the very real power dynamics, violent systems, and oppressive behaviors of our fellow humans.

A séance is defined as an attempt to communicate with spirits or the dead, often through the support of a medium. A séance can also be utilized to communicate with our shadows, our ego, our saboteurs, and our inner children. In many ways, therapy and coaching work is an ongoing séance or communion with these parts of ourselves. However, not all of us have access to one-on-one work with professional space holders (or mediums). And more, even if we do see a professional regularly, doing this work in our own time and with our own communities is a necessary skill to develop when cultivating fulfilling relationships.

We've discussed that relationships are informed by power

---

4   I'm choosing to use the word séance because I'm a witch and I feel aligned with this language. But I'd like to note that we can also use words such as conversation, meeting, check-in, communion, session, gathering, discourse, or discussion. Any space in which feelings are encouraged to be shared honestly and power dynamics are acknowledged as we seek to unsettle and reckon with them.

dynamics. Identifying the power dynamics at play is the first step, but certainly not the last. If we identify a power dynamic, we can then work to destabilize or accept this dynamic. There may be situations in which a power differential is necessary, such as a therapist holding a safe container for their patient. But, if patients don't feel encouraged to name how the power dynamic is working, it may cause more harm than good. In order to reckon with a power dynamic we need to both remove biases and inequalities and enact reparations and equity. In the book *Relationship Anarchy: Occupy Intimacy!* Juan-Carlos Pérez-Cortés explains, "any relationship model that aims to be ethical must have at its very core an analysis of power relations and proposals aimed at changing them" (2020, p.54). It is not enough just to acknowledge our biases and discuss inequalities. We must also work to replace unethical power dynamics with consensual, mutually beneficial dynamics. There is no predetermined script for what these beneficial dynamics will be. We each must collaborate with our partners and communities to figure out what feels right.

WAYS TO COLLABORATE WITH OUR PEOPLE WHEN EXPLORING POWER DYNAMICS

1. Identify your role in the power dynamic: In what ways do you hold power or not? How do you experience the power and privileges of others? Do you feel encouraged to offer feedback on how the power dynamics are playing out? Do you feel open to receiving feedback about your impact on others? You may want to openly name your positionality in a dynamic.
2. Normalize conflict: If something is off, let your humans

know. Encourage your people to do the same. Practice taking space and returning to the relationship. Can you identify the difference between healthy conflict and signs of abuse? Hold this question close as you navigate power.

3. Ask open-ended questions: How does our dynamic feel to you? What do you experience in your body when you're with me? How can I support you to let me know when something feels off? How would you receive feedback about something you did that hurt me?

4. Share your boundaries: Let people know what you expect in relationships. Let them know how you'll respond if they can't treat you with respect. For example, I expect people who interact with me to use my correct pronouns; if they can't do that, then I'll let them know our connection can't grow beyond acquaintance.

5. Own your privilege: It's okay to be transparent about what you have experienced and what you don't know. Don't be afraid to acknowledge the way privilege and power have shaped your worldview. No one expects you to be perfect, so don't expect others to respond to your mistakes perfectly either.

6. Notice your energy cycles: If you're feeling drained or exhausted, pay attention. What is sucking your energy? Are you exhausted in a satisfying way or exhausted in a perpetual burn-out kind of way? What can you do to replenish energy? These cues can offer information about the kind of dynamic you're in—if you feel burnt out and exhausted, you might be experiencing a harmful power dynamic. (This is why most of us in the world feel burnt out a lot!)

7. Practice humility: Expect to make mistakes. Notice

what making mistakes feels like. Pay attention to shame and self-hatred. Reach out to safe people when you do fuck up, so you can learn from what happened.

8. Take up space: You deserve to be here. Dance, sing, write, make art, critique ideas, discuss with friends, destroy things, build things, love people, try something, be messy, be human, be here.

9. Acknowledge that we have different tasks: Someone with a lot of privilege may need to practice cultivating humility, whereas a person who experiences marginalization may need more practice setting boundaries or taking space. Don't assume your journey is the same as anyone else's.

When collaborating with the people in our life, it is important to center and attune to those who are most marginalized. I recently had a colleague share with me that my attempt to destabilize power and privilege had actually reinforced my power and contributed to their feeling of being unheard. They shared with me that I was enacting anti-Blackness by centering my own attempt to support them, instead of centering what they needed at that moment. While I absolutely went through my own process of immense shame and guilt for making a mistake, I was and continue to be profoundly grateful for the care that is required to tell someone how they harmed you. There is nothing else to do in these moments except receive the information and integrate it as deeply and profoundly as we can.

During this experience, I began to reflect on the moments in my life in which I have chosen or not chosen to communicate the impact of someone's actions because of their position of power. I felt an immense softening as I touched into the part of me that genuinely cared that I had hurt someone, and I genuinely wanted to change my behavior so the mistake wouldn't happen again. Perhaps if I cared this much about my actions, could someone else care about their impact on me? It takes so much courage to share the way you've been harmed, and this sharing should not be taken lightly.

In Tina Mattsson's article "Intersectionality as a useful tool: Anti-oppressive social work and critical reflection" (2013), she describes a three-part approach to identifying and exploring the way power dynamics and oppression are impacting a social work context (social workers and clients). This approach can be adapted to help us explore power dynamics in our relationships. And after all, social work is a work of relationships, even if the terms of the relationships are quite different from romantic, friendly, or familial.

This three-part approach begins with identifying an incident and describing it with as much detail as possible. Imagine a situation or dynamic as a prism; as you turn the prism you can see the shape from many different sides. As you look through the prism at different angles, the perceived world changes too. In this step, you might ask someone you love to sit down and talk about all the details of a situation together.

To create this container you want to:

1. Set up a time and place to talk; be clear about how much time you have to talk.
2. Encourage honesty and gentleness. If one of the people has been harmed, encourage them to be honest. If one of the people has caused harm, encourage them to be gentle.
3. Keep asking questions. Centering the person who is harmed or experiences more marginalization, stay

curious. Try questions like: How did that impact you? What happened next? What else is important to share?

The second step of this approach is to "make a critical reflection on your description" (Mattsson 2013, p.13). Within yourself or with someone else, explore the power dynamics and oppressive systems that may be impacting this situation. Consider how the parties involved are viewed and portrayed relationally. Are some people considered deviant? Who is considered a reliable narrator? Who is believed to have the capacity to report the truth and who isn't? Are there concerns about safety or danger related to specific people? How does the relationship uphold normative beliefs and systems related to race, class, gender, ability, and so on?

Mattson's third step addresses how we move forward. What will we change? What needs to be tended to, held, or acknowledged? Be specific about what you will change. If you're in a position of power, try to avoid blanket statements like "I'll do better," or "change is happening." Think about what needs to change on an internal, interpersonal, and systemic level. You may not be able to transform everything, but you can make movement within yourself. As you embark on change, consider the timeline of this transformation. You might ask people in your community how long they think something should take. For example, unlearning transphobia is often a lifetime project for cisgender people. There are, however, landmarks that let us know we're headed in the right direction. Think of something you can do today, this month, this year, and this lifetime. Today, you might be able to share your experience with someone you trust so you can get support for ongoing change. In a month, you might be able to read a book on queer and trans history. In a year, you might be able to become an expert at using they/them and neopronouns. In a lifetime, you could contribute to trans movements by protesting, donating, and helping educate others.

A huge part of this work involves attuning to our emotional and physical responses in our relationships. In a society founded on ownership, coercion, and manipulation, it will undoubtedly be difficult to find other ways to relate to each other. That's why it's important to see this process as a process. We may make a small adjustment, hoping to disrupt a power imbalance, and find that our adjustment led to the creation of another power imbalance. It's okay to feel dejected by the insolvable quality of this work. It can be helpful to think of this work as a living, breathing organism. We don't expect our bodies to be fully satiated forever after one meal! Nor should we expect our social and interpersonal conflicts to be resolved with one intervention. I invite you to stay with the experience, shifting and adapting as new information arises. I often heard the mantra repeat in my head: What does it feel like now? What does it feel like now? What does it feel like now?

SOMATIC TOOLS

This work invites an engagement with our bodies. As Moss described in our interview, one of the most pivotal aspects of exploring non-normative worlds is exploring our internal world. Moss expressed how important understanding our nervous systems is to developing fulfilling relationships.

It seems like we can't forget the nervous system. I think the thing that I'm excited about is the way that we stay in our bodies with this information, the way that we are in community and building and playing with our communities, but [while] holding this information, does that make sense? Like, not discounting the ways we need to learn how to regulate. Just because we know theoretically that, yeah, I wanna build this smorgasbord[5] with you that has all these really interesting pieces and the sky's the limit, that is *one* part of it. And the other half is gonna be how does that land in my nervous system, being in a body with you, while we practice this together? So I think that's the thing that I'm excited about as this conversation continues through our collective, how are we going to get deeper into our bodies and embody the shit out of this?

One of the greatest tools we have in relationships is practicing curiosity. Our bodies give us information: Defensiveness, fear, and resistance are all key pieces of information. As we dive deeper in relationships that exist outside social scripts, we will embark on more unknown territory. If you are a human, you may already know that our bodies often experience change as threatening.

When we feel threatened our bodies activate a simple nervous system response to help us address the threat. Our nervous system can't differentiate between a "real" or "perceived" threat; it is one and the same. Further, the way our body decides to respond to threats somatically is largely out of our control. We can notice our system utilizing fight, flight, freeze, or fawn responses, but we can't stop them from happening once they've started.

Our fight, flight, freeze, and fawn states describe four ways

---

5   Moss refers to the relationship anarchy smorgasbord, which we will
    explore in Chapter 4.

our body automatically reacts to perceived threat. In a fight state, blood surges and our heart rate quickens. You might feel angry, aggressive, or a desire to punch something. In a flight state, the body engages our muscles and we experience an impulse to get away. In a freeze state, the body may become numb and motionless, you might have a desire to lie down or curl into a ball. In a fawn state, the body may try to suppress emotions in order to focus on placating another person. This can look like agreeing with someone to avoid further conflict or acting sweet so that another person doesn't stay mad. Oftentimes, the body tries out different approaches to a perceived threat to see what works. For example, in an argument between two people, one person might respond to the conflict by getting angrier and louder (fight state). But, if fighting back isn't effective at mitigating the threat, the body may switch to a fawn response by suddenly agreeing with the person they were just arguing with. Can you identify a time you felt each of these responses? Can you recognize when each of these states is happening?

I find Deb Dana's explanation of polyvagal theory in her book *Anchored: How to Befriend Your Nervous System Using Polyvagal Theory* (2021), to be an immensely helpful entry point into understanding the changing world of our nervous systems and bodies (see Figure 3.3). There are three basic elements of polyvagal theory: the autonomic hierarchy, neuroception, and co-regulation. The autonomic hierarchy describes the process through which our bodies process information, moving in a specific direction and operating with specific responses. The autonomic hierarchy begins with the ventral system, which is the state in which we move throughout our day with calm, where we connect with others, and find flexibility when challenges arise. If our body senses that our ventral system isn't up to the task to help us navigate a situation, our body will switch to our sympathetic system. Our sympathetic system, which helps us fight and run away, is full of big active energy. If we keep exerting this big energy and we can't find relief, our body will switch into a dorsal phase. The dorsal system helps us lie down, give up, and repress our desires. We need all of these systems, and they help us throughout each day of our lives. Can you notice what system you might be in right now?

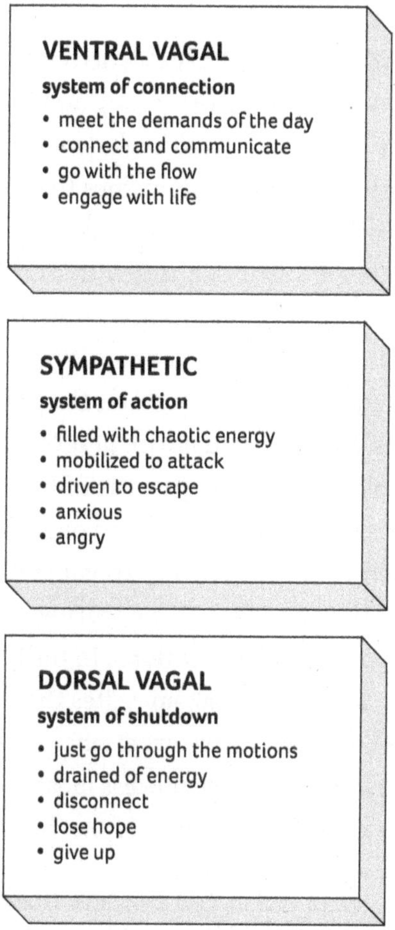

VENTRAL VAGAL

system of connection

- meet the demands of the day
- connect and communicate
- go with the flow
- engage with life

SYMPATHETIC

system of action

- filled with chaotic energy
- mobilized to attack
- driven to escape
- anxious
- angry

DORSAL VAGAL

system of shutdown

- just go through the motions
- drained of energy
- disconnect
- lose hope
- give up

Figure 3.3 Three building blocks and emergent qualities

As I write these words I can tell I'm in my ventral vagal system because my breath is even and slow. When my dog interrupts me, I feel calmly available to respond to his needs. I feel mostly comfortable and at ease in my body. I can feel that I'm on the edge of my ventral vagal system because I know I could jump up and start solving a problem right now if I needed to. My breath is even now, but there is an edge of tightness in my chest like a little anxiety creeping in. This shows up in the form of typing quickly and checking the time as I write, eager to be productive.

If you like moving around, try this activity: Set a timer for five minutes. Put on your favorite song and move your body in any way that feels good. Notice whatever it's like to be in your body. Which polyvagal system does this feel like? When the timer goes off, turn on an upbeat, dance-y kind of song. Dance to this song for five minutes with as much energy as you can muster. Jump around, spin, run, anything you want. Notice what this feels like in your body. When the timer goes off, pause the music. Now, lay down on the ground in silence for five minutes. What do you notice here?[6]

Somatic exploration is the process of becoming curious about what it *feels* like to be you. It is an ongoing process, one that can deepen your relationship to yourself and through that, to others. However, it is also a journey that will invariably stir up big and complex emotions. In the book *My Grandmother's Hands*, Resmaa Menakem writes that "The body, not the thinking brain, is where we experience most of our pain, pleasure, and joy, and where we process most of what happens to us. It is also where we do most of our healing, including

---

6   This activity is adapted from Deb Dana's work and Michal Rokach Shamay's interpretation of it during a Therapeutic Communication class at California Institute of Integral Studies in 2023.

our emotional and psychological healing. And it is where we experience resilience and a sense of flow" (2017, p.38). The body is a great resource and companion, and it can also be a confusing source of information. As you begin to tune into your somatic experience, be mindful of the judgments and stories you tell yourself about what bodily sensations mean.

As you embark on your relational journey, I encourage you to think about an artistic medium that might help express your inner experience without words. There is so much to say about our emotional experience, and so much more that cannot be said. This work is, at its core, about expanding our capacity to hold and identify multiple things at once. As we explore the depths of our somatic experience, we will come across things that are confusing or contradictory. How do we hold space for ourselves through this growth?

When I asked partners Nazeil and Ethan about the tools they use to navigate relationship anarchy, they both recalled the insightful reflections of Jessica Fern on healing attachment wounds. Fern speaks to the lifelong challenge of transforming our brains and bodies to meet our attachment needs, rather than relying on outdated coping mechanisms we developed in response to our childhood environment.

One of the greatest challenges I face in my coaching work is balancing this growth with a container of safety. I hold space for my clients to challenge their coping mechanisms, while also honoring that wherever they are today is okay. This kind of nuance is difficult to hold. It requires expansion in our bodies and minds. We must become stretchy, able to hold the way we are *currently* responding to our partners, friends, and loves with the way we would like to respond to our partners, friends, and loves. This is aligned with a therapeutic practice called dialectical behavior therapy (DBT), a modality developed by Marsha M. Linehan to help support folks with borderline personality disorder, although it has also been beneficial for folks with post-traumatic stress disorder (PTSD), complex post-traumatic stress disorder (C-PTSD), and many other folks who aren't struggling with these specific mental health challenges. The basic theory of DBT is that we can hold multiple conflicting realities at once. We can affirm that we are okay as we are today, and that we are working to change certain behaviors and patterns that aren't working for us.

Nazeil and Ethan shared another important reflection towards the end of our interview: the concept of resisting the desire to "fix" things by taking a pause and taking space. Ethan explained:

> For somebody like me who is the doer and the caretaker, the most challenging and most healing thing sometimes is doing nothing. Like, absolutely not acting, not responding, asking for a moment to take some space and not doing anything at all. And letting those moments pass. And then no damage has been done.
>
> Nazeil: Yes. Just like time, literally a time thing. Like literally just wait it out.
>
> Ethan: And slowing down, not fixing things. Allowing people to take care of themselves.

We live in a culture of urgency. Capitalism requires us to get up earlier, work harder, and stay longer to produce more and make more money. And yet, as humans, sometimes slowing down is the most effective solution to our struggles.

Slowing down is one of the most powerful somatic tools we can use to create relative safety in an unsafe world.

What pace do you take in this world? Do you feel an urgency

to get things done? Do you find that slowness is hard to find? Or perhaps you notice people speeding around you, moving faster than you can keep up with? What would you like to do more slowly?

On that note, I encourage you to pause here and go do something that feels good for at least five minutes. Take some deep breaths, jump around, eat a snack, or check yourself out in the mirror!

BEFRIENDING THE SHADOWS

As you continue to embark on the journey of relationship anarchy, you may discover parts of you that are less than enthusiastic about the way your relationships are developing. These parts may feel jealous, angry, resentful, or mistrustful. They will likely arise to try to protect you from getting hurt from other people. It's common for monogamous people to say, "I could never have multiple partners, I'd be too jealous!" This can be painful to hear if you're a non-monogamous person who experiences and navigates jealousy, as most of us do. Further, most monogamous people feel some amount of jealousy in their lives as well. The goal isn't to avoid or eliminate these feelings, but to befriend them. This is something we can do in any relationship.

Alaina Knox (they/she) is a queer, fat, Black, non-binary shadow worker. I asked them to explain their experience of doing shadow work, and how it could benefit those of us embarking on journeys of relationship anarchy.

Shadow work is the process of tending to that which is pushed into the subconscious. Some people think that it's inappropriate to suggest that just a regular common civilian person can do shadow work, without a licensed professional. I don't think that's true. I think that Indigenous communities have had ways to tend to the invisible and things that are not super tangible and not right there in the conscious, before psychology was a thing. What is pushed into the subconscious are things that are not acceptable. So we're split between the part of us that wants to be our authentic selves and then the part that wants to experience belonging. Belonging is a core human need. This is important for relating to each other because...I don't know, because, we suck, honestly. As a species, we are really mean to each other and we don't have very many introspective practices. We're mirrors to each other. Our life usually reflects what's happening internally which is very controversial for a lot of people, and in part for myself, because of systematic oppression. I am actively in conflict with it because it's like, white supremacy. And, I just cannot deny the ways that I've *seen* myself over the last few years since I've been engaging in this practice [shadow work]. And I guess the thing is, white supremacy teaches us that we're not worth shit. You know, I used to be a part of this community and they would say that white supremacy taught us how little a human needed to stay alive, with slavery. And we internalize this and then we're like, I don't deserve shit. And so then without knowing it, we're playing out this limited belief that we don't actually deserve good things or pleasure and that we need to be in a competition to figure out how we can survive off the least, you know.

Shadow work invites us into this question: Is it possible to acknowledge the impact the system has had on our brains and bodies without feeding further into the system's power? Does revealing the way we've contorted ourselves to be accepted cause more harm, or more possibilities for liberation?

Shadow work can help us reveal the patterns and narratives that keep us stuck in cycles of suffering. I'm reminded of this drawing done by Marcos Alvarado. The image shows a human skeleton struggling to drag a large, lumpy bag across the ground. Underneath it reads "before therapy." Below this image is the same skeletal figure dragging their lumpy bag, but there are angry demon-like shadows emerging from the bag. The figure seems to be struggling slightly less. Underneath it reads "during therapy." Finally, we see the figure walking hand in hand with the demon-like shadows, who have smiles on their faces. They are all at ease. While we can come to befriend our shadows in many ways, aside from therapy, this image illustrates the shift in burden that occurs when we release our shadows from a trapped and obscure place. Shadows can even become companions, offering insight and guidance as we embark on the journey of life.

Our shadows help us identify our motivations and our desires. To feel and see parts of ourselves that we are scared of is undeniably uncomfortable, and sometimes overwhelming, but it is incredibly informative. Let's look at jealousy. Is jealousy an emotion? A sensation? A story about what's happening in a relationship? When you experience jealousy, what happens in your body? What kinds of thoughts do you have? What impulses arise?

Jealousy is not as simple as we are often led to believe (by society and by our own brains). It can be a manifestation of fear, insecurity, envy, desire, and/or grief. It can be a mild, uncomfortable experience or an earth-shattering physical and emotional state. There is no one quick fix for navigating jealousy because it is a uniquely personal and relational experience.

In many intense emotional experiences it can be helpful to combine approaches that soothe the conscious/thinking and the subconscious/body. One of my favorite tools in this regard comes from Eve Rickert (2014). We can delineate jealous feelings from jealous actions. Jealous feelings are out of our control—they can arise when our body perceives a threat to our relationship or well-being. Jealous actions are within control of our conscious mind and body. A jealous action might be telling a partner to cancel their date or ignoring a partner without communicating what we're experiencing. It is also possible to respond to jealousy with non-jealous actions such as requesting a check-in, asking for help, allowing tears to flow, or letting someone know we need space. The actions you choose will be dependent on what you've co-created with the other people/person in your relationship.

Consider these three approaches to jealousy. Which one do you tend toward? Which one might you like to try?

1. Jealousy arises as a felt sensation in the body coupled with thoughts about how and why your needs could never be met. You take a breath. There is a welcoming of emotions. You ask another human for space to process and explain why you're feeling jealous. They're not available right away, so you give yourself permission to feel upset and scared. It's a very hard couple of days, but you find ways to be kind to yourself during that time. You're able to check in later about what happened with your person, and you continue the process of exploring why you responded that way. You feel compassion and understanding towards your jealousy. You lay a soft hand on the place you feel the most intense sensation, and let that part know you are there.

2. Jealousy arises as an overwhelming flood of panic and fear. Your brain is spinning out of control with thoughts and stories about how you'll be left, abandoned, or hurt. You feel certain other people cannot be trusted, and you want to keep yourself safe. It feels impossible to stay in connection and feel this much emotion, so you deny and suppress your emotions. The feelings get too big to deny when you're with your person, so you take some space, aware they are confused about how you're feeling. Your partner feels hurt and rejected, which you experience as further proof they aren't safe for you. The feelings eventually subside, but the idea of talking about it is too overwhelming so you try to move on until the cycle repeats.

3. Jealousy arises as intense physical and emotional over-whelm. Your immediate thought is that your person is making you feel this way, which is really hurtful! You let them know that they're hurting you and that they need to change their behavior in order to keep you safe. Your person wants to support you, but they don't feel like they're doing anything wrong. They know they love you and are committed to your relationship. You express your feelings more and louder until your partner agrees to make whatever was making you jealous go away. You feel some intense relief, but it doesn't last long. Soon there is another situation that activates these same feelings. You feel like you have to work overtime to make sure your person doesn't do or say anything that might make you jealous.

All of these stories make a lot of sense to me, and I've certainly tried each of these approaches. My goal is not to shame or judge anyone for the way they're coping with life on this Earth. I do, however, want to offer tools that may relieve suffering. So let's start exploring some of those!

ANCESTRAL SUPPORT SYSTEMS

As we've discussed, relationship anarchy, as a practice, has been around a long, long time. Because of this, we can all draw on ancestral human traditions to inspire and guide our relationships. Mora Miller offered this perspective as a way to create meaningful bonds between ourselves and other humans. They asked the questions, "Who are your ancestors?" and "How can we lean into our own indigenous origins as a resource?" Mora spoke to the importance of naming our teachers, our guides, and our histories. Their reflections remind us that part of our relational work is to name and own how we arrived at this moment in time. This includes taking responsibility for the power we hold as well as honoring the ancestors who have survived for us to exist. As I am a white person, most of my ancestry is rooted in the violent traditions of colonialism and white supremacy. It feels important to hold this reality in my day-to-day life, acknowledging that white supremacy has been both traumatizing to me and to everyone I interact with. I can also feel into my ancestors who were marginalized, ignored, or forgotten, especially my queer, trans, disabled, poor, and non-white ancestors. The spiritual and relational practices of the people who have lived before us can inform the way we move through the world today.

When I speak of ancestors, know that I don't necessarily mean people who you are genetically related to. You may consider the people who were integral to the communities you inhabit to be ancestors, or even the authors who wrote your most cherished books. Consider, which humans can offer you guidance and wisdom as you navigate this world?

The ancestors who come to you may not be the ones you think you need. After a recent conflict with a friend, I found myself seeking insight from ancestral beings. I settled down into my bed and began reflecting on the people who have come before me. I imagined their lives, their bodies, the way they might have loved. I thought about the food they ate and the sacrifices they made for me to exist. There is a long history in my family of abusive and alcoholic men. I couldn't stop thinking about these men, who had suffered so much from generations of Catholic patriarchy and abuse. I could see their faces softened by death, and I felt aware of their humanity. Despite my own complex relationship with my father, I felt a kind of unconditional love for and from the fathers in my family. I remember thinking, *these are humans who knew about fucking something up.* It was a strange feeling, but I felt at that moment that there wasn't much I could do that would make these ancestors stop loving me. They were living in shadows, grief, hatred, and harm, and in death they were no longer afraid of those dark places.

Che Che Luna (they/them) is a queer, trans, chicanx sex + pleasure educator, movement storyteller, and sensual embodiment facilitator. They spoke to me about their journey of discovering ancestral knowledge in their body and community. I asked Che Che, "How did you come to connect with your ancestors? Have you always had a relationship with your ancestors?" Their response:

As someone who does not have access to my extended family, due to homophobia, my connection to my ancestors has required daily devotion to researching, (re)learning and reclaiming. There was a point in my life around age 30 where I realized that a sense of belonging was not going to come from someone or something outside of myself. This realization helped me take charge in cultivating what I was deeply longing for—home, connection, and love. I really started to understand that the wound I carried of being severed from my culture, my homeland, and my ancestral knowledge was not just mine, and that the majority of the people around me were experiencing this pain of disconnection and colonization too. The most powerful threads that have reconnected me to my ancestors have been dance, music, food and recipes, altar building, intentional rituals and ceremonies, connection with the elements, and building chosen family.

In what ways does your life incorporate your ancestral knowledge and connections? If you have little or no knowledge of your ancestral origins, what kinds of traditions would you want to create in the present? Ancestral wisdom challenges the idea that there is a fixed human relationship to time. In many ways, our younger selves are the ancestors of our present selves. What might you learn from returning to the dance, music, food, recipes, symbols, play, ceremonies, nature, and chosen family that were most meaningful to you as a child?

Che Che further echoed this ever-present resource of ancestral support. They explained, "The wisdom of my ancestors lives both in my body and in the more-than-human world around me. I am in the ongoing practice of orienting and listening to that steady loving support that is always available to me. My ancestors have taught me and my community that we are never actually alone." I wonder what is possible when we begin to undo the myth that we must be alone in order to be strong? Che Che reminds us that in interconnectedness, we find liberation. This doesn't mean, however, that we can claim others' bodies as our property. They explain, "My queer, 2spirit, Indigenous transcestors know and embody a way of living that centers respect, consent, and generosity over ownership, entitlement, and scarcity. Their relationships to land, loved ones, and all living beings are a constant source of guidance and remembering for me."

A simple way to engage in the cultivation of ancestral wisdom is to receive and honor the stories of people who have come before us. Think about who you admire or respect in your family, in your community, or in the world who is even a day older than you. This could include animals, plants, or other celestial beings. Invite this being to share their story with you, taking special care to receive their experience with openness and generosity. You may choose to ask someone you know personally to share their story, but this invitation may not be so direct. It could look like reading a memoir, listening to a podcast, or watching a documentary. As you prepare to take in the wisdom of this other being, try to imagine them eating, breathing, or moving as if they were right next to you.

Finally, I invite you to consider what kind of ancestral knowledge you'd like to leave on this earth and in your communities. How do you want to be remembered? What kind of change do you want to be part of?

Think about the humans who you will become an ancestor to, whether or not they are blood relations. What kind of world would you like to create for them? What insight, wisdom, or support would you like to offer them?

CREATING INTIMACY AND CONNECTION

If we want to build deep, complex relationships we must utilize our human capacity for connection. Connection can erupt spontaneously between people or be cultivated with intention. There is no one flavor of connection and no one pathway to finding it. Why are we drawn to certain people? Why do we feel seen by some and not others? And why is it that some connections last and some fizzle out?

For someone who spends many hours every week meeting with people in relationships with each other, I still feel quite amazed at how varied human relationships can be. Some people find joy in going to festivals together and creating wild, unique art. Others yearn to snuggle up with their pets and be blissfully alone from human interaction. Many humans crave a little bit of all kinds of connections, dreaming of stable long-term partners and flirtatious comets[7] they see once a year.

There is certainly something ephemeral about human connection. Dating apps with algorithms that match humans up together based on interest love to report their success at pairing up humans, but many of us have experienced first hand meeting someone who seems like they will be perfect for us, but there's just no spark. Or they're too similar! Or they're great in lots of ways but completely incompatible in just a few, essential ways. Or they simply came along at the wrong time and we weren't ready to receive their love.

My grandmother has always said to me, if you are open to love, it will come to you. But what does being "open" to love mean? Let's explore together some of the qualities that can

---

7   Partners who enter into our lives infrequently, but are deep and meaningful connections. For example: a friend who visits twice a year for a weekend of cuddling and forehead kisses.

develop and deepen connection and intimacy, the ways we can stay open to love and invite relationships.

Play

Quite a few studies in the last sixty years have illustrated the value of play as a pathway towards connection.[8] Playing with other humans improves our communication, our ability to navigate conflict, our relationship satisfaction, and our relational bonds. Play can also promote creativity, spontaneity, and reminders of the positive connection partners share. When humans have fun together they experience relaxation, positive emotions, calm, and openness to collaboration. When humans are able to play together they're more likely to be able to navigate conflict and disagreement. Some studies have even found that enjoying another's company in the way one does with friends is the most important factor in determining the overall sense of satisfaction in a romantic relationship.

If you want to incorporate more play into your life, think about the things you genuinely enjoy doing and then look for opportunities to do them with other people. This could include board games, erotic exploration, sports, dancing, karaoke, playing with animals, rock climbing, crafts, book clubs, or meme-sharing!

Honesty

Honesty is the best policy, right? That's what they say! So why is it that so many of us struggle to be truly honest with

---

8   Aune and Wong 2002; Baxter 1992; Betcher 1977; Kopecky 1996; Lauer and Lauer 2002; Markman et al. 2004; Vanderbleek 2005.

ourselves, our partners, our lovers, our friends, and everyone else we come across? Honesty is vulnerable. Being honest requires revealing our actual desires, which many of us work hard to keep secret. If we keep our desires secret, we can protect ourselves from the pain of rejection, being misunderstood, and/or not getting our needs met. Sometimes we have a clear understanding of what our needs are, but we choose to misrepresent or conceal our truth to protect ourselves. I find even more often, we don't *know* what is true and honest. When working with couples, I have found that asking "What do you need from your partner?" is one of the hardest questions for people to answer. Many of us are not given the space or tools to learn about what we want and need. In fact, many of us are trained from a young age to suppress and silence what we want and need. Identifying our feelings can bring up panic that we will be punished or rejected, especially if this mirrors our prior experiences with parents or caregivers. To be honest, we must know what is true for us. So how do we learn about what is true?

Intimacy with self

If you want to be open to love with others, there is a simple place to start, with the self. There is so much we can understand about our love for others when we turn inward. In our own bodies and brains we can discover our motivations for connection, our desires, our pleasures, and our relationship to love.

There are so many ways to turn inward. Whatever path you decide to embark on, notice which practices feel easeful and sustainable. If you try to force yourself into a reflective practice that you hate, it is much less likely to be supportive and meaningful than a practice that genuinely brings you joy. On the other hand, sometimes the exploration of self we need involves cultivating discipline and habit. I encourage you to play with your practices, tweaking and updating them to fit your needs, instead of falling into rigid patterns that aren't truly helpful.

Many people find journaling to be a portal to self-understanding and compassion. Have you ever tried journaling? What was your experience? What feelings do you notice as you consider journaling as a pathway to self-exploration?

Let's start by discussing two different journaling prompts and why they might be helpful.

Prompt Number One

- Write down everything you did today (or yesterday). Just the cold hard facts. Once you've finished, start again and write down just the emotional content of the day. How did waking up feel? How did breakfast, work, chores, and all the other moments of the day feel?

This prompt is supportive for those of us who have trouble remembering what we experienced. If you find it hard to hold onto the tasks, thoughts, or feelings that make up your life, you might benefit from this kind of journaling prompt. This prompt is also helpful for those of us who need a straightforward place to start. If you're feeling stuck, come back to the basics. What did you do today? And what was it like for you? In the realm of self-knowing there is no insight that is too mundane to give attention to.

Prompt Number Two

- Set a timer for 15 minutes. Free write about how it feels in your body. Use whatever images, descriptions, verbs, or even drawings you can think of to describe your somatic experience. You can even include drawings, collages, or other visuals.

This prompt is helpful for those of us who can get overwhelmed by the intensity of our inner world. If you experience a lot of sensation in your body, it might be helpful to process your internal experience with words and/or images. Is it possible to befriend the intense emotions that move through you?

Self-exploration doesn't have to be a solo endeavor. We can learn more about ourselves through discussion with others. Talking with friends, going to therapy, or joining a support group are all ways we can learn more about our internal landscape. If you're a verbal processor, meaning you tend to understand things better after you've talked about them, you might benefit from this kind of self-exploration. You might also consider creating a self-dialogue practice in which you speak out loud to yourself or record yourself speaking and listen to your words.

There is also so much to be learned from the body that is non-verbal. Through movement, meditation, and mindfulness we can cultivate our awareness of the visceral and somatic elements of our experience. Taking even one minute a day to notice your breath and become aware of your physical body can be transformative. If you find it hard to sit still for long enough to meditate, you might try moving or dancing as you pay attention to the sensations in your body. Consider how you could express your inner experience without using words. How would you breathe in a way that honors sadness, anger, or joy? How can you move to deepen your closeness with your heart and lungs? Where does vibration, heat, and tension live in your body?

Wherever you feel drawn in your self-exploration, cultivate an appreciation for the unique journey you are taking in this life. Relationship anarchy offers us a portal to self-knowledge and autonomy by resisting the narrative that we can own or be owned by other people. In relationship anarchy we are free to pursue pleasure in a way that makes sense to our bodies. When we receive this gift of freedom, we must also consider how we facilitate freedom in the people around us. How do you support the self-exploration of your friends, lovers, and community? Do you honor and make time for everyone's self-exploration? Is alone time valued? How do you affirm others' right to self-exploration?

It is not uncommon for relationship anarchists and solo polyamorists[9] to find common ground. Both of these relationship approaches affirm the importance of autonomy and self-expression. And, there is ongoing dialogue in relationship anarchist and non-monogamous communities about how we can avoid leaning too far into self-centered approaches that negate our inherent interconnectivity.

Mora Miller shared with me their process of finding the balance between self and connection with others:

I was polyamorous for years. I think the most partners that I

---

9   A style of non-monogamy that often involves maintaining social, emotional, or physical autonomy in ways that go against traditional romantic relationship norms. For example: a solo polyamorist might live alone and have a separate bank account from a long-term partner.

had at a time, not that I'm counting it up as like a body count or anything like that, but I wrangled four for a hot minute, which is extreme. And I learned so many lessons as some came in, some went out and some of 'em stacked up all on top of each other 'cause they were running at the same time. And realizing that one of the key tenets is, oh, love is abundant. But people aren't, time isn't, energy isn't. And when you run out of those things and you have committed or you're in a relationship with somebody, it's very unfair to them to be like, oh yeah, I'm gonna take you on too. And then it turns into like polyamory Pokemon and you're like trying to catch 'em all and like hurting everybody in the process, which is utter bullshit and really unethical.

And that's when I started to realize that like, okay, the ethics underlying all of this are actually far more important than how you actually do it. And that was my first glimpse into relationship anarchy without even actually having the terminology for it. When I started realizing that how you do this and how you treat other people and how you live your life ends up being far more important than the labels that we use. So, practice ends up being the most important thing.

I went from being polyamorous to being solo polyamorous because that was my path to egalitarianism. What I was not realizing was that it was my hyper individualism talking and it was colonial culture being like, "Oh, I'll just get all these privileges and I'll just be able to live my life on my own terms and I won't have to commit to anybody or do anything that I don't wanna do." And sweet. I get the best of all the worlds. I'm still polyamorous, I'm still independent and I can do whatever I want and like blah, blah, blah, all this stuff. And I did that for years and some people were like, I totally get it, or whatever.

And then I met some other solo polyamorous people and I

was like, you guys, I hate to say the S word, but y'all are a little selfish. This is really weird. Like, I thought we cared about ethics. I thought we cared about how we treat each other and like not just communicating what we want and how we wanna be, but not using people and not just using people to check off a box or meet a need or whatever. Like they have needs too. And they're just as valid and like it's polyamory. We love them, we care about them.

Mora came across solo-polyamorous people who were practicing in a way that was misaligned with their approach to relationships. But that doesn't mean that solo-polyamory is inherently bad or unethical! In fact, I think many of the values of solo-polyamory go hand in hand with relationship anarchy. However, in all relationships we have to negotiate our own personal relationship to what is ethical and what is misaligned. Mora's journey illustrates the real-time negotiation they did in order to honor their autonomy and care for other humans.

This is the crux of human relationships: How do we find what works for me and what works for you? How do we balance autonomy and interdependence? How do we sense imbalance in ourselves and in our relationships and course-correct when needed?

In order to muddle through these questions we must find ways to communicate our experience and deeply listen to the experiences of others. Let's dive into exploring the nuances of communication and how it can facilitate deeper intimacy, connection, and understanding.

CHAPTER 4

Collaboration and Co-Creation

Communication from the Beginning

It's a popular refrain in the non-monogamous world to say that love has no limits, but time does. One of the biggest challenges I experienced when first exploring relationship anarchy was scheduling! Scheduling work, sleep, hobbies, alone time, dates, friend time, and check-ins, I felt pushed to my limit. I had to reorganize expectations of my week, clarify my boundaries around sleep and me-time, and communicate with partners what they could expect from me. I also learned to get creative about how I connected with people. Nowadays, I don't always have time for a hangout with everyone I love, but I make a concerted effort to connect in some way with my humans every week.

In new relationships, it can be helpful to normalize direct communication right off the bat. Consider starting your new relationships (of any kind) with a conversation about your needs and wants in relationship with each other. This might include asking:

- What kinds of activities do you want to do together?
- How much time do you have each week for hanging out together?
- What other relationships are in your life?
- What are your hopes and dreams for the future?
- What sort of vibes do you want to cultivate between us?
- How do you want to feel when we're together?
- What are your preferred methods of communication?
- How quickly do you respond to texts?
- How do you want to be held if I do something to hurt you?
- How will you respond to feedback that you've hurt me?

It would probably take a very long time to talk through all of these questions in one conversation, but these are great things to think about and discuss while you're getting to know someone! You will probably learn about a new person's qualities and preferences naturally over time. I have a new friend who started regularly sending me audio messages instead of texts. Conveniently for me I love receiving audio messages, but sometimes it takes me longer to listen to them because I need a quiet, private place to listen. Knowing this, I took a moment to tell this friend exactly that. "I love receiving your audio messages, and as a heads up it may take me longer to respond to them than texts. So, if it's urgent feel free to text me and say 'listen now!'"

It is small moments like this that build into one big house of direct communication and trust. We build this house of communication so we can hold conflict and joy as it arises. In an interview with Moss, they described conflict in relationships as "a healthy, normal, and potentially sacred part of building relationships." Even though we so often attempt to avoid conflict, it's hard to imagine a deep, fulfilling relationship without it. Conflict opens potential for intimacy. It can be lovely to connect with people who we never have conflict with, but often this means staying on a surface level when it comes to trust and closeness. Clear communication facilitates, and even celebrates, conflict. As you continue practicing your communication skills, think about your willingness to be forthright with new people in your life. It is undeniably counter-cultural to be direct with someone you just met, and it's incredibly vulnerable. Consider these questions as you explore your relationship to new relationships!

How honest am I willing to be about what I want with a new person? Am I open to navigating conflict early on in order to clarify our expectations? What is my relationship to rejection? How open am I to finding out someone doesn't want to be friends/partners/lovers with me?

EXPLORING DEFINITIONS, TERMS, AND LABELS

There are endless possibilities for human relationships. Part of the reason I love relationship anarchy so much is because it offers a mindset towards relationships that can be tailored for *you*. One of my favorite relationship books on this subject is *Designer Relationships* (Michaels and Johnson 2015). Mark A. Michaels and Patricia Johnson define a designer relationship as a relationship that entails "free and enthusiastic choice, mutuality in defining the relationship and establishing parameters, permission to consider all forms of relating, dedication to maintaining radical regard of your partner(s), [and] regular testing of the nonexclusive for sexually transmitted infections (STIs) and transparency about sexual history" (p.3). This mindset of relationships reminds us that beyond some simple ethical agreements, so much is possible! Terms and labels are tools. We get to determine the bounds of our relationships from the definitions we create, rather than the terms and labels that seem like the closest fit. If our terms don't help us describe our relationships, then we don't need to use them! We can create new terms, squish terms together, or just let go of some terms all together.

Just a few terms we might use to describe relationships are: sweetie, lover, friend, comet, partner, husband, wife, babe, love, girlfriend, boyfriend, mother, father, sister, brother, cousin, auntie, uncle, guncle, sparkle, ankle, Daddy, Mommy, Zaddy, Domme, Dom, sub, baby, pet, owner, beau, spouse, mistress, soulmate, significant other, boo, bae, cutie, queer platonic partner, best friend, bestie, acquaintance, colleague, frenemy...

Continue this list! Which terms do you use for people in your life?

Let's step away from all the terms for a moment and think about *your* relationships with some more intention. I invite you to choose one relationship in your life to explore. Let this be an opportunity to practice thinking about how you relate to other people in your life. Later, we'll use the relationship anarchy smorgasbord as a collaborative tool to identify needs and wants *with* other people. But first we're going to gather information about someone in your life and how you feel about them.

- What do they like to be called? What do you like to call them?
- How did you meet them? What was your first impression? Has it changed since then?
- How often would you like to see them? What would you like to do with them?
- How do you feel about this person? How might you describe your feelings for them? Where do the feelings live in your body?
- Would you call this person in an emergency? Would you call them if you received good news?
- Do you ever feel sexual desire for this person? What do you crave?
- Do you ever feel romantic desire for this person? What would feel good?
- Do you feel desire to have platonic or friendly touch? What kind of touch would you want from this person, if any?
- How much of yourself do you like to share with this person? Do you feel comfortable being messy, weird, or silly?
- How would it feel if your relationship with this person changed drastically?

Okay, let's pause for a moment because that's a lot of questions. I want to start by inviting you to notice how these questions make you feel. You can take a moment to close your eyes or soften your gaze and pay attention to the sensations in your body. Notice your chest, your heart, and your shoulders. Is there tenseness or softness? Notice your stomach, your pelvis, and your thighs. Any squeezing or clenching?

How does breathing feel? Easeful or tense? Do any of these questions feel really lovely to ask? Or are there any that feel uncomfortable to ask?

As we explore the relationships we want to develop, we will touch against emotions and sensations. This information can help us understand how we are experiencing the present moment. When exploring our relationships with others we might find ourselves eager to make sense of things or create new, clear relationship structures—that's okay! If you notice anxiety coming up, you might get curious about slowing down and staying in the unknown. Without jumping to conclusions, let's keep exploring how words can help us describe our relationships in playful and unique ways. We can discover definitions outside of heteronormative scripts!

Let's explore how you relate to these terms and who in your life might be included in them. After each term, consider the questions and write down your definition of the term. Feel free to include drawings, poetry, song, or dance to describe the vibe of that label. If you want, you can also create your own terms for people in your life. Combine or make up words that make sense to you!

Friend: What is a friend? How do you know someone is a friend? List some of the people you consider friends. Do they have anything in common?

Partner: What is a partner? Is it different from a husband, wife, spouse, girlfriend, boyfriend, or sweetie? Do you have people in your life you consider partners? Do they have anything in common?

(Chosen) Family: What makes someone family? Who is part of your family? How might you make a family tree? Are these people blood related or not (or a mix)?

Romantic friendships: Do you have any friends you feel romantically interested in? Do you have friends who you enjoy holding hands with, going on dates with, or doing other things you consider romantic?

Partners who don't live together: Do you have partners you don't live with? What is this like for you? Are there partners you've had in the past or currently who you'd like to live separately with? Would you want to live in separate houses, rooms, states, or countries?

Co-parents: Do you have someone who helps you raise animals or humans? Does this person have other relationships with you aside from co-parent?

Comets: Do you have any lovers, friends, or partners who you see occasionally, perhaps once a month or once a year? Comets may be occasional connections, but they can still be deep and meaningful. Are there people you'd enjoy seeing every once in a while?

Does a husband need to be a romantic partner? Does a wife need to be someone you're married to? Can a partner be platonic? Can you have many soulmates? These questions can be extremely validating and/or disorienting to ask. Many of us have been trained our entire lives to not ask these questions. Some of you may even find these ideas to be laughable! I can hear a voice in my head that sounds a lot like a crotchety judgmental lady saying, "A platonic partner!? That's absurd!" And yet, I have a platonic partner who I love dearly every day. Whether these voices come from in you or around you, it is a reminder that pushing against the norm is a weighty burden. As you look below the surface of social norms, you may find that what is true is not always easy to acknowledge or accept. For example, the implications of realizing that your chosen family understands and sees you in deeper ways than your biological family can be huge. What are we willing to risk in order to live our lives authentically?

In relationship anarchy, we are invited to get clear on why specifically we want others in our life. If we feel a desire to get off the relationship escalator, we might find the floor we land on to be a little shaky. What do relationships mean outside the labels of husband and wife, partners, family, or soulmates? We may still choose to use these terms for people we love, but rather than applying these terms to people automatically, we can collaborate with the people we love to choose the terms that are right for the relationship.

For example, I think it's fun to use terms like wife and husband for people in my life. I recently started a Future Queer Parent club with a friend of mine. She hosted our first meeting and went all out with snacks and drinks. At the end of the night, I gave her a hug and said, "Lyla, you are such a good wife to me." We gave each other a peck on the lips and giggled playfully.

I also have a partner who I have been with for four years who I occasionally call my husband. Recently I lovingly called them "husband" and they raised their eyebrows at me. "I don't know if that fits anymore," they said. I felt a little bit sad, because I like using that term for them, but I know there are lots of terms I like for them, so that sadness felt possible to hold with care. This became an opportunity for us to discuss and update the terms we like to use. To be clear, their feeling that "husband" didn't fit wasn't related to their desire for commitment or intimacy. We ended up deciding that "spouse" felt more authentic.

We can use labels as tools. They help express how we feel about our people, rather than delineate the kind of relationships we have with our people. If they stop feeling right to anyone, we can collaborate on what feels authentic right now.

Questions to ask about labels and terms:
- How do I feel about [blank] as a label?
- What kinds of images, sounds, feelings, and thoughts does it evoke?
- Which labels are important to me?
- Which labels feel trivial?

IDENTIFYING COMPATIBILITY AND AFFINITY

In our first interview, Mora Miller posed a profound question, one that they ask themself when making new connections: "Are we in affinity or not?" What a poetic way to ask about compatibility! Compatibility is not a fixed quality in a relationship. We can be aligned in some ways, and very incongruent in others. At some points in life we may have space for lots of differences; at other times, we may need close humans who share similar identities and life experiences. One of my favorite things about humans is how magical and ephemeral compatibility and connection can be. Sometimes humans from totally different cultures, backgrounds, languages, and life experiences feel uniquely drawn to each other. They might embark on lifelong connection, perhaps learning different languages or cultural norms in order to share more parts of their lives. Other times humans may seem extremely compatible, sharing similar beliefs, goals, or values, but find that they just don't really get along. I once had a queer, non-binary, kink, and sex positive therapist who I felt regularly misunderstood by. I assumed that because we shared certain identities, they would be a good fit for me. When it came to their therapeutic approach and their personality, I found it just wasn't what I needed at that point in my life. Now I have a therapist who is quite different from me, and we've done deep and meaningful work together. We seem to *get* each other. It works for me to have a therapist who doesn't share all the same identities with me, but that's a specific kind of relationship. I can imagine it could be difficult for me to have a long-term and deep partnership with someone who doesn't share core identities, but I'm also open to the possibility that it's completely possible; it just depends on the person.

How do we identify if we are compatible with another person? First, we have to consider what our boundaries and expectations are in different kinds of relationships. For example, I have an expectation that anyone I am friends with can communicate with me about their feelings, boundaries, and needs in our relationship some of the time. I don't need anyone to be perfect, as I myself am not perfect. I use my internal emotional information to track how much conflict I'm able to hold. It's very difficult for me to be friends with someone who is regularly passive aggressive, defensive, or uninterested in personal growth. I'm cool with friends who act this way sometimes, but I rely on my internal compass to let me know when it's gone too far.

Cleopatra Tatabele (they/them), a Black and Indigenous Two-Spirit change-maker, spoke to the importance of having clarity about your needs and wants in a relationship.

I have learned to fucking stick with what I want. I just had a friends-with-benefits breakup and the person was like, "Do you wanna be friends?" I thought about it and I had to grill them a little bit. Like, "What does a friendship look like to you? Because I don't even know if that's a good fit for me because friendships look like emotionally really caring and that's not what you've been able to provide and what I want in my life is emotional care from my friends. So like, is that something that you do? I don't know if you could provide that" and they're like, "No, I don't think it's gonna work out." Sometimes people just default to, oh, this is the type of relationship that I guess we can settle for. But, you don't have to settle for relationships at all. I know for some people boundary setting can be really uncomfortable, but it's incredibly important to only allow people in your life if they align with what you want in your life. I think that's been a really big lesson for me. Not compromising and allowing people in my life when they're not good fits. I've had people who have wanted very different qualities than me and that was not something that worked out. Like, I'm a very free love person. I've had people who are like, we can only have open relationships where you can get with someone but you have to break up with them in two months. That does not work for me. I've had people who are like, "don't ask, don't tell" type of relationships. That does not work for me either. I don't like that. It might work for other people, but I am very kitchen table. I've had people who are like, we only date people together or we don't date anyone at all. I like my autonomy, so that does not work for me. And so it's like people, as they date, as they figure out what their polyamory looks like, really go with your gut and like, don't settle for things that will make you uncomfortable and unhappy long term.

Cleopatra's experience of determining compatibility has been a journey of trial and error, exploring different relationship styles and then updating their relationship preferences based on how they experienced these different relationships. So much of determining compatibility comes from lived experience with another person. Compatibility is not something we can always define with rigid boundaries; there is often a gray area, something left to be discovered. At the same time, we can use our lived experience to make well-informed decisions about what works best for us. Cleopatra emphasizes the importance of believing ourselves when we discover something is not a good fit. We don't have to settle for something that we don't want. It is always okay to say, "That may work for you, but it's not going to work for me." And of course, things change! What works now won't work forever. It's okay, perhaps necessary, to shift and update our preferences and boundaries.

I once took an amazing workshop with Dr. Liz Powell, an esteemed sex educator and therapist, on building non-monogamous relationships. They asked us to explore our "dimensions of desire." They outlined a whole list of different aspects of relationships, from level of kinkiness to level of sex drive to level of relationship structure. When we discussed relationship structure, they explained that on one end we have relationships that have very defined rules, expectations, and agreements with very little spontaneity. On the other side, they described a free-form relationship that had no specific expectations beyond communicating about safety. Everyone in the group took a moment to place ourselves on the line between these two styles. I'm including this section of the worksheet below so that you can do the same (Figure 4.1).

After we placed our mark, Dr. Powell asked us if our answer

would change if we knew we would be safe in the relationship. Would you change your level of relationship structure if you knew you could be safe? What would change for you if you felt more security with other humans?

For many of us, exploration feels more possible when we feel safer. Many of us use rigid structure and rules to help ourselves feel safer. If we tell ourselves and our partners they're not allowed to leave us, then maybe they won't.

There's nothing wrong with seeking safety in life. For many of us, the insecurity that comes with more free-form relationships can be so dysregulating that it's counterproductive and unhelpful. My hope is that we can utilize relationship anarchy practices and approaches to support and enliven all our relationships, even ones that are very structured or rigid. There are so many ways to be a human in this world. Our only task is to find a way to be human that is supportive to ourselves and those around us.

As our relationships develop we will inevitably be invited into updating the amount of safety or risk we're comfortable with. Compatibility with others changes as the relationship and our lives change. If you find someone in this world who you are compatible with I invite you to keep asking the question: How are we compatible today, this year, this lifetime? How does our compatibility change depending on the other factors in our life? How has our compatibility changed over the course of our relationship already?

As compatibility changes, we'll need to update the relationship structure we create with others. This is a creative and evolving process that will continue to surprise you. For now, let's consider what kind of relationships might work for us, and what we ultimately are seeking when we reach out to build connections with others.

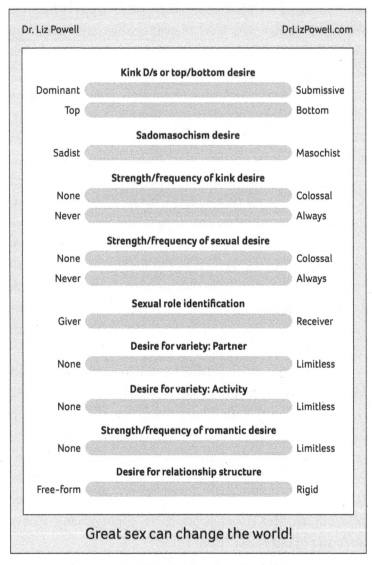

Figure 4.1 What does my desire look like?[1]

---

1. Please note that while we changed the formatting of this worksheet to be congruent with the rest of the book, this worksheet was created by Dr. Liz and has been generously shared to be included in this book. To find more of Dr. Liz's worksheets, go to drlizpowell.com.

RELATIONSHIP TENDING

Relationship anarchy is an expansive way of relating to others, but it doesn't mean we can do whatever we want all the time. It's important that we keep up with how our relationships are doing. I like to think of this as a process of tending. One of my partners once described their meditation practice as a process of regular housekeeping. In order to avoid doing a huge, messy clean every once in a while, we can regularly sweep the floors and dust the window sills, keeping things manageable. The same is true with relationships! If we incorporate weekly, monthly, and/or yearly check-ins into our lives, we can stay up to date with fluctuating needs of our relationships.

Not all relationships call for weekly check-ins, but most relationships benefit from yearly (or even bi-yearly) check-ins. You might think of a longer once-a-year check-in as a deep cleaning or reorganization. During a relationship check-in we can get clarity on how things are going, if anything needs to change, and how everyone wants the relationship to proceed.

To introduce a check-in, ask someone in your life if they have time to talk about the relationship. Here are some examples of inviting this conversation:

I recently learned that it can be valuable to do friendship check-ins once a year and talk about our goals. Would you want to do that with me?
I'd love to hang out with you and talk about how our relationship is going. I think it would be really nice to get more info on what we both need.
Would you want to start doing weekly check-ins so we can stay updated on scheduling and plans for the week?

I'm thinking of doing a yearly relationship review and making some goals for next year. Would you want to join me in that?

During a check-in, be mindful of creating a container that facilitates openness and honesty. You might want to start with the same opening question like: How are you feeling right now? Or: What color would you pick to describe how you feel today? You might also consider ending your check-in with the same ritual. A handshake, hug, or high five can be a good way to mark the closure of a conversation. This kind of repetition can be soothing to our nervous systems. Even if the conversation itself is scary or unknown, creating a simple routine to start and finish provides security and builds trust.

During the check-in you might want to have a list of what you need to go over, such as "scheduling, non-monogamy updates, things that went well, things to improve." This meta-list should reflect the needs of the relationship. What do you need to talk about? For housemates this might include "house things," whereas long-distance partners might include "planning for visits."

During your check-in, think about how you can provide the most comfort and support to everyone involved. This might include doing your check-in in a room that feels comforting, making sure you have eaten and had water that day, or celebrating what a good job you're doing at your check-in as you go along. If you can, make your check-ins something to look forward to! If you see your check-in as a chore, you might want to pay attention to any resistance you have to the check-in, not to override your resistance, but to get more information about what is happening for you.

While check-ins can be tiring and time consuming, they are also a crucial part of relationship building. These conversations are the groundwork for all the fun, sexy, and playful parts of a relationship. In order to feel safe enough to explore pleasure, we need to make sure we're on the same page logistically and emotionally.

A beautiful aspect of relationship anarchy is the commitment to freedom and the pursuit of connections. That doesn't mean that we get a free pass to do whatever we want without keeping our partners updated (unless that is an explicitly agreed upon dynamic). A weekly check-in with romantic and sexual partners can help us stay updated on who our people are seeing so we can negotiate and re-negotiate our expectations as well as set boundaries for ourselves about how we want to interact with the relationship.

Many of us felt a different weight to our responsibility to others when the Covid-19 pandemic first surged through our communities in the winter of 2020. While many non-monogamous people were already having conversations about safer sex practices and sickness transmission, these conversations spread to the general public. It became acutely obvious how interconnected we all are. While it may seem burdensome to constantly update people on our exposure to illnesses (including STIs) it is a crucial element of disability justice and ethical relationships. The reality is that disabled people are regularly excluded from communities and relationships because their accessibility needs are seen as burdensome. If you are an able-bodied person navigating this world I invite you to consider: In what ways can I maintain my autonomy *and* affirm others' right to know their exposure to illness? How can I honor my need for independence without denying others' need for information? Where is the line between pursuing what I want and ignoring the feelings of those around me?

There is one simple way to address these deep questions:

Be as forthcoming about your activities as you can. Share honestly with the people around you about what you're up to. You don't need to give away all the intimate details of a relationship to share useful information such as "I exchanged bodily fluids with this person," "I'm becoming interested in seeing this person every week," or "I went to a play party and I didn't wear a mask." These updates are valuable when it comes to physical safety, but they are also a way to tend to the emotional safety of a relationship.

Relationship anarchy is not a free pass to do whatever you want without consequences. If you're seeking partners who have no interest in sharing information about what you're doing or who you're doing it with, that is your prerogative; just be very clear you're on the same page about it! For those of you who crave partnerships that include sharing of lives and experiences, you'll have to navigate the realities of communicating about your sexual, romantic, friendly, and familial relationships.

Remember, you get to decide what you're okay with in relationships. If you find yourself in a relationship with someone who seems uninterested in communicating clearly about the actions that impact you, it is okay to set clear boundaries about how you connect with them. Prentiss Hemphill said in an Instagram post, "boundaries are the distance at which I can love you and me simultaneously." It can be immensely painful and challenging to identify the exact distance at which we can both be loved, but it is a loving thing to strive for. Even boundaries that limit our time and connection with someone to very little interaction are loving. To share with another human the terms required in order for you to love them wholeheartedly is a sacred gift. Someone else may not see it that way; that doesn't negate the loving effort of a clear boundary.

EXPLORING THE WHY OF RELATIONSHIPS

To help you consider what might be right for you in your relationships, let's start by asking why you're in relationships at all! I invite you to take five to ten minutes to respond to these questions in the margins of this book, a journal, in a voice memo, or in a conversation with someone else:

What is the point of a relationship?

What do different kinds of relationships bring to your life?

Do you crave certain kinds of relationships?

Do you crave certain activities with other humans?

When do you seek alone time?

When do you seek time with others?

Notice how it feels to ask and answer these questions. What is it like to feel your body as you consider the kind of relationships that would be ideal for you? Do you notice hope, dread, fear, or excitement? What cues does your body give you to help you identify these feelings?

There are as many relationship approaches as there are relationships. Each combination of people will come together in their own unique way. And we can see over-arching traits and commonalities that help us describe the kind of relationship we want to experience, which is helpful so that we can find the other people who want similar things. However, many of us inevitably discover that what we thought we wanted, or what a partner thought they wanted, isn't actually what is needed for them at that moment in time. Whatever relationship configuration we are drawn to, we must grapple with the reality of this universe: Change is constant.

When we are clear about the *why* of our relationships, we can use this to center ourselves through change. Consider this: You embark on a romantic relationship with another human who you love spending time with. Being in their presence is a joy. You laugh together, you share similar interests, and you feel like a solid team navigating the challenges of life. After some years of loving each other romantically, you start to notice that your relationship is shifting. You don't crave romantic connection in the way you used to. Things you used to find romantic, like kissing, having sex, or sleeping together, feel like less important parts of your relationship. You and your love check in about where things are, and you reckon with the reality that while you still love each other, you're not romantically in love in the same way you were some years ago. What now? You start talking about what you *want* to keep doing together and what you're ready to let go of. The conversation is painful and you notice a lot of grief. It's hard to let go of this romantic connection. Through it all you're aware that you don't want to lose this person in your life. You still laugh together, you still share many similar interests, and somehow, even through this grief, you're a team. The *why* of your relationship is that you genuinely enjoy each other's company. You begin to ask: What is possible for us if there isn't romance here anymore?

I share this example because it is one I have come across countless times in my personal and professional world. There is no guarantee that we'll be able to transition relationships from one format to another, but knowing our why is helpful regardless. The why of each relationship will feel a little different. Sometimes we embark upon relationships because we have a shared goal, like starting a business, having children, or leaving an unsustainable family dynamic. Other times our goals are not so clear, or we have multiple overlapping reasons for being in the relationship.

We may not always be able to uncover every nuance of why we're relating to someone, and that's okay. I simply invite you to stay curious about what you're receiving from, and what you're offering to, other people.

In our current cultural paradigm, straightness, cis-ness,[2] and monogamy are non-consensually required of all humans. The idea that you could actively opt into a relationship rather than being forced to practice it, is radical. People who practice non-normative ways of being and loving are intimately familiar with the requirement to be intentional and clear about what they want in a relationship. We have learned through trial and error, and the wisdom of those who have come before us, that no relationships can thrive without boundaries, agreements, and mutually agreed upon ethics. What is true is that in relationship anarchy there is a lot more freedom about what these boundaries, agreements, and ethics will be. In the space of this freedom we come up against miscommunications, confusion, and hurt. We often find that our values are not entirely aligned with other people we care about. It can be helpful to explore alone and with our people how we define an ethical relationship. How do we delineate between discomfort and harm? How do we determine what feels supportive? What is the boundary of what we'll tolerate in a relationship?

---

2   The qualities or traits of being cisgender.

These questions must go hand in hand with asking why we're in relationships, because they help us bring the why into a tangible reality. This process may be a somatic unfolding, an exploration of our physical and emotional responses to the experiences of our life. We can begin to ask these questions of our body: When do I feel safe? When do I feel access to pleasure? When do I feel able to embrace the complexity of my human experience? What am I doing here, on this earth, and how do I want to spend the time I am given here?

We may also be called to ask: What do people owe me? And what do I owe to others?

WHAT DO I OWE TO OTHERS?

Throughout my interviews, I heard quite a few people express ambivalence, uncertainty, or downright skepticism about the ethicality of relationship anarchy. Yael explained to me her complex experience of relationship anarchy.

It might just be I'm hearing the wrong people, but the way that I've heard some folks talk about relationship anarchy, I'm like, no, that I don't agree with... There are people who *are* more important in my life than other people. Not because of the status that they hold, but because of the connection that we have. My love is expansive. And also, there are people that I love more continuously, more consistently, more deeply than others, just 'cause I'm not in relationship with every person I meet to the same degree. And I've heard some weird descriptions of relationship anarchy where people are like, "Oh, they hang out more with them and they see them as more important in their lives" [in a judgmental tone] and it's like, yeah that makes sense to me—relationship nurturance, which can come in different forms, has an impact.

Yael is speaking to a common interpretation of relationship anarchy that any preference or hierarchy between partners is unethical. Hierarchy is a controversial topic in the world of non-monogamy. Some feel passionately about deconstructing hierarchy in all its forms, others choose to incorporate hierarchy with consent and intention, and some use hierarchy as a way to control and manipulate people. I believe there are ways to engage with hierarchy that can ethically co-exist under the umbrella of relationship anarchy. Humans who take a non-hierarchical approach to their relationships often exemplify the values of autonomy, independence, and non-possessiveness. Also, it's possible to allow preferences and boundaries to emerge from the needs and wants of the people in a relationship that reflects a consensual hierarchy. In my mind, the most important factor is informed consent and acknowledgement of power differentials.

A good example of this is "unicorn-hunting:" the practice of (often) straight, cisgender couples seeking a third to have sex with or casually date with the caveat that this third person can be expelled from the relationship at any time and has no real say about how the relationship goes down. This kind of hierarchy is harmful and unfair to a third person entering a relationship with an assumption that they will be incorporated into the relationship with care, mutuality, and a similar level of intimacy. However, if the terms of the relationship are clearly defined, and everyone in the dynamic has an informed understanding of how it will go down, including information about how they will each behave if things are no longer working, there is no reason to be alarmed. What I'm describing is different from unicorn-hunting because it's a mutually agreed upon process. The third person gets to fully consent into the circumstances without being led on or manipulated. There are plenty of self-described "unicorns" who enjoy stepping into a couple's dynamic without the responsibility or intimacy of a more serious relationship. The issue arises when people aren't clear about what they're looking for and what they're able to offer.

In my interview with Andie Nordgren she described how important it is to affirm our individual right to create relationships that work for us. She noted that as a younger person she sometimes fell into the trap of believing that relationship anarchy is a more enlightened relationship style than non-monogamy. I asked her, what changed? How did she come to believe that any relationship style might be okay?

I don't know, I feel like I mostly want to attribute it to growing older and having more experience with life and people. And, I think that the main understanding is how many constricting factors there are on people's lives, other than relationships. And, for some people what is important for other people is not important. Surviving in capitalism, there are many other things that are bigger on people's agenda and so this is one topic in the thousands of topics that can govern life. I mean, sure, it's a pretty big topic for most people, like, how their relationships work and how they organize their lives. But, I think also there are probably a lot more radical things that you could do to transform a society than your own relationship practice. But it is also radical. So both of these things, all, can be true at the same time. I think it's the more boring, grown up version of all of this, right?

And I think for me the thing that can never be unseen or walked back from is this idea that you don't have a right to control another person. And I think that was one of the things that most pissed me off with monogamy, right? That people would come into it with this entitlement to controlling another person. Like, "I'm right. And I have a right to control what you're doing." And I have a right to essentially bully you into the condition of my love that I must have. Otherwise it's like I boot you from love to not love. Regardless of how you structure your practical life, right? I mean, I happen to have two kids with my wife and you know, we are married because of international shit that is important when you have kids and come from different countries. But that doesn't mean that we are monogamous. These are material realities that we have to structure our life around but completely fundamental is this idea that again, I have no right to control anything with her. That the foundation of all of the important relationships in my life is that fundamental idea that we want to give each other agency and we do not feel entitled to any control of the other person.

In all relationships, it's important that we fill our own cup as well as those of the people around us. Relationship anarchists include our relationships to self as part of the web of love that fills our lives. In relationship anarchy we affirm that romantic relationships are not inherently the most important relationships in our lives. But for some of us, romantic relationships are the most important relationships in life. This isn't less evolved or less valuable; it's reflective of the reality of some human emotions and experience. That is what relationship anarchy is all about: supporting humans to make the choices that work best for them.

THE SMORGASBORD

Take a moment to imagine a big wooden board covered in all your favorite treats and snacks. Cheese, olives, fruit, bread, jam, cured meats, butter, and candies. Your mouth waters as you imagine all the flavor combinations possible. Where to begin?

The relationship anarchy smorgasbord is a visual tool that can help us identify and articulate what we want from a relationship. Just like a smorgasbord of snacks, the relationship anarchy smorgasbord can be sampled and utilized in so many different ways. Take a second to look at the smorgasbord in Figure 4.2.[3]

In the first circle of the smorgasbord we have the categories Power Exchange, Kink, Physical Intimacy, Emotional Intimacy, Domestic, Romantic, Sexual, and Partnership. Under each of these categories are a few examples of what we might discuss when exploring this category. It's easy to see that these categories are not strictly defined or static. Emotional Intimacy and Physical Intimacy can certainly relate to Power Dynamics, Kink, and Sexuality. Domesticality and Romance for some is

---

3   The hosts of the podcast Multiamory reference an article by Sue Sutherland titled "Your Relationship Needs a Blueprint", in which the origins of the smorgasbord are cited, stating that Lyrica Lawrence and Heather Orr of Vancouver Polyamory created this concept in December 2016 (Lindgren et al. 2021). This article has since been deleted, so it was difficult to verify this information. It can be challenging to track who first coined a term or discussed an idea, this is why I strive to name everyone I've heard of and acknowledge that many people who have been pivotal in developing these ideas are not named. If you or someone you know has knowledge or memories about the history of relationship anarchy, please reach out! I'd be so curious to hear your thoughts. Since its conception, the smorgasbord has been updated and revised many times.

related to Partnership. This model offers us a starting point to explore how these things relate for us and the people we relate to. Some folks may find that Domesticality and Romance are completely unrelated to their Partnership. Other folks may focus on Kink and BDSM but disregard Romance completely.

Rather than being a replacement for the relationship escalator, the smorgasbord is a practical tool for co-creation. In an episode of the podcast Multiamory, the hosts discuss the way we might use the smorgasbord as a tool for discussing the parameters of our relationships (Lindgren et al. 2021). Dedecker Winston, one of the hosts of Multiamory, helps guide our thinking with a series of questions: "Do we have shared accounts or shared financial responsibilities? What communication frequency do we want? Do we want daily, do we want monthly, do we want it inconsistently? How do we feel about legal entanglements? Does that include things like marriage, adoption, being the executor of my will? And so on and so forth."

Dedecker illustrates just how deeply we can explore these topics. While it can be both overwhelming and inspiring, we are offered a pathway to create our relationships, and sometimes we find that the labels that currently exist can't contain the complexity of our relationships. Dedecker speaks to this in the podcast episode: "I think for me, looking at this chart, [it] becomes really clear about how our traditional labels of friend, romantic partner, acquaintance, and stranger, doesn't quite cut it. It doesn't cut it out clearly how we're actually connecting to each other. I guess the ideal use case with this chart is that I can sit down with somebody that I'm just getting to know and maybe we both expressed an interest in creating some intentional relationship together."

Relationship Anarchy Smorgasbord: a tool for discussion

This board includes a number of concepts antithetical to many understandings of relationship anarchy.

Not all who use this are relationship anarchists, and are those who are may need to discuss how their relational style differs from cultural norms.

The categories are loose generalizations to help conversation, and are arranged with those relating to the larger social/political systems toward the outside, and the more personal toward the center.

Suggested notations: Yes, Maybe, Maybe in the Future, & Let's Talk. Definitely No. Color-coding and highlighting are fun too!

To form your relationships: You and another can pick any number of "items" from any number of "platters," take a huge helping or just a scoop. The dish the two of you hold is your relationship. Remember you must agree together on what is in it! No sneaking items in without the other knowing or there will likely be conflict or disappointment later. Also: it's your dish, so if you decide to change what you want from the smorgasbord later, that's cool.

Legal
Power of attorney
Business Partner Adoption
Marriage Executor of will
Civil partnership

Collaborative
Teaching projects
Organization

Power/Hierarchy
Boss–employee
Sponsor–sponsee
Teacher–student Mentor/guide

Exclusivity
Sexual Emotional
Social Structural

Caregiving
Health Sponsorship Reliability
Emergencies End of life/death
Receiving care from
Giving care to

Religious/Spiritual
Shared ritual/prayer
Shared beliefs Discussions

Professional/Work
Combining social and collaborative
Colleagues Partners

Emotional Intimacy
Being vulnerable Love languages
Sharing values/beliefs

Physical Intimacy
Dance Cuddles Hugs
Pets Massage Hand-holding
Nudity Kissing Co-sleeping
Body contact

Labels/Terms
Chosen family Spouse Parent
Cousin Sibling Datemate

Systems of Oppression
Race Ability Gender Class
Skills Influence Citizenship
Financial Sexual orientation

Domestic
Routines Chores
Sharing a dwelling/home
Sharing a sleeping space
Cooking together Sharing meals

Romantic
Cultivating uniqueness
Emotional attraction
Shared experiences
(going on dates)

Kink
Sadomachism Sadism
Fetishes Masochism

Creative
Visual art Music Yoga
Craft Acrobatics Dance
Comedy Improv Martial arts
Theatre

Financial
Money Payments
Shared accounts Responsibilities
Property . Support

Sexual
Kissing Orgasms?
Involving genitals, anus
Chemical reaction Body touch

Partnership
Shared goals, values
Commitment Routine
Embracing change

Power Exchange
Age play D/s
Pet play M/s

Co-caregivers
Family (sick, elderly)
Animals Plants Children

Communication
Frequency & Method Daily
Weekly Monthly Annually
Inconsistently In person
Phone Text Written

Companionship
Playfulness
Shared activity/interests
Intellectual/philosophical
Discussions Friendship

Emotional Support
Listening Empathy
Being asked for advice Confidante

Public Displays of Affection
Events Friends Family
Work Social media Seen together

Originated by Lyrica Lawrence & Heather Orr of Vancouver Polyamory in December 2016 (v1). Updated by Maxx Hill with the guidance of the Relationship Anarchy, Polyamory, and Solo Polyamory Facebook groups: April (v2, v3) & September 2018 (v4), & January 2019. This is Version 5. Please share. Translations into any language are welcome. Contact Maxx for editable file: maxhillcreates@gmail.com.

Figure 4.2 Relationship Anarchy Smorgasbord

The smorgasbord is a tool anyone can utilize to begin or deepen a conversation about what you want to do together. Many folks enter into marriages with expectations of each other they don't even realize they have. There are some great resources out there in the form of "questions to ask before you get married," or "questions to ask before you have kids," but oftentimes these resources assume that you're only going to have *one* conversation before this big life event. What if we assumed that a relationship was a living, breathing contract that could be changed and revised as needed?

In Chapter 1, we heard from Andie Nordgren about the origins of relationship anarchy in the creation of live action role playing games. Andie explained that "the magical circle"[4] is a social contract that determines the expectations of the game play. She explained that her experience in participation-focused art practice was one of the entry points of considering relationship anarchy. Here she elaborates to include how this process of creating a magic circle relates to creating relationships.

You have monogamy, a very strong magic circle, where either you're in it or you're not, it's a specific set of agreements that you kind of enter into that come as a package. And the moment you start working with these agreements, with people, as a kind of design medium, you immediately hit questions of power, right? Who has, who gets to have, a democracy and that's where the anarchism comes in. Because this was also a community and a practice that had anarchist activism ties and, so on. But from the angle of questioning

---

4 The magic circle is a concept from game studies that describes the way agreements and expectations change during game play (Linser et al. 2008).

those power dynamics, the anarchist principle is that *those who are affected by something should have influence over it.*

Our smorgasbord can help us define a magic circle. What are the guidelines, agreements, and expectations of our relationships? I would encourage you to look at the smorgasbord with someone in your life and talk through the different aspects of your relationship that you see represented. What is missing? What had you already considered and what is revelatory?

The smorgasbord helps us visualize the theoretical approach we are taking to relationships when employing relationship anarchy values. Everything is out on the table, and we can clearly see what our options are. With the help of the humans we are in affinity with, we can make combinations and experiment with new configurations. If you are someone who needs clarity and structure, you might consider writing down all the elements of the smorgasbord that you want to include in a relationship and then fleshing out what each of these elements includes. This can become a kind of breathing contract, something contained, yet mutable, that helps people understand what to expect from each other.

ORIENTATIONS TO SEX

One of the many delicious treats to choose from the relationship anarchy smorgasbord is the kind of sexual exploration we want with others. The way we orient our bodies, hearts, minds, and spirits to sex is as varied as the way our universe creates living beings: infinite and expanding. Relationship anarchy is a relational orientation that may be a good fit for someone of any sexual orientation or proclivity. It is the expansive nature of relationship anarchy that supports differences in sexual desire and attraction.

Relationship anarchy invites us to focus on people's needs without judgment or shame. There are so many ways to be human, it is inevitable that we will find ourselves in relationships with people who are different from us. It is not uncommon for people to reach out to me looking for relationship coaching because they are experiencing mixed desire[5] in their relationship. Mixed desire is the experience of having such different needs for sexual, romantic, and physical care that it's causing distress in the relationship. But this doesn't have to be a death sentence for love. What if we were open to a relationship that was authentically compatible for the people involved, instead of trying to fit a structure onto humans for whom it doesn't apply?

What is your relationship to your sexuality? How often do you crave sexual touch? How often do you crave orgasms? What kind of sexual play brings you joy? How do you experience pleasure?

The term megasexual describes people who experience sexuality, sexual desire, and sexual expression as intrinsic to their sense of self. Sharing their sexual self with others is a necessary part of the way they get to know others, and how they let others get to know them. A megasexual person might feel especially unseen or unsupported in a relationship that doesn't include some kind of sexual energy exchange. Of course, this is not so over-arching that megasexual people can't experience fulfilling nonsexual relationships. However, many megasexual people consider their sexual relationships to

---

5   This is also sometimes called "desire discrepancy."

be integral parts of their life, self-expression, and experience of community.

Conversely, the asexual spectrum describes a diverse group of people who have some, little, or no interest in sexual expression. Someone on the asexual spectrum may experience sex as a casually fun thing to do with friends, rather than an important declaration of love and commitment. Some asexual folks don't experience any sexual attraction, but may enjoy genital pleasure because it feels good. Masturbating next to a friend might feel more aligned with a person's needs. Juan-Carlos Pérez-Cortés writes that, "for those in the asexual community, relationship anarchy is important because it is the only approach that offers a way to combat allosexism, meaning that it removes sex as an indicator for and measure of a relationship's value" (2020, p.47). Have you ever felt pressured to have sex with a partner to prove that you love them and are committed to them? Sex can be a joyous way to play, but it doesn't need to be a core aspect of relationships in order for those relationships to be meaningful. If there was no pressure to have sex, can you imagine the kind of relationship to sex you might cultivate?

There is also a pervasive cultural belief in the US that sex with people who aren't romantic partners is less important, deviant, or harmful. Consider how taboo it is to pay for sex, when this is a completely valid way to get sexual needs met. Paying someone to provide sexual pleasure might be helpful if you don't have a current sexual partner who can meet those needs, but it's also something that anyone should feel encouraged to do as long as they're being ethical, consensual, and considerate. Many people also feel uncomfortable with the idea of sharing sexual energy with a friend. I once had a friend who I went on a long trip with, in which we shared a lot of hotel rooms. After several weeks we finally broached the topic of masturbation. "Why don't you go take a walk and I'll masturbate and then we can switch?" they offered. I was so relieved that we could talk about it openly and get our needs met. After we both masturbated, we rated our orgasms on a scale from one to ten, just for fun.

Have you ever felt sexual feelings for a friend? What kind of sex do you like to have? Do you like to include toys, role play, or kink? Do you prefer sex alone or sex with one or more people? Have you ever paid for sex or porn? What is the best sex you've ever had?

While our sexual desires exist within our own bodies they are also informed by our relationships with other humans. It is possible for humans with vastly different sexual landscapes to have fulfilling sexual relationships with each other. This all depends on our capacity for navigating differences. So often in our society we have been taught that difference is shameful. Especially in our sexual and relational orientations, if we find that we relate to the world very differently from the people we love it is understandably alarming. Will our differences be accepted or used against us? Is there a right and wrong way to be? Having two different approaches to something like sex is not necessarily a dealbreaker. It is possible to find the space in which our Venn diagrams of desire overlap. It is possible to hold the differences in our desire with reverence and care.

In situations of mixed desire, when partners have different sexual wants/needs to the extent that it's causing distress in the relationship, it is possible to negotiate and accept our unique sexual landscapes. This requires radical honesty about what we want, curiosity about what's possible, and an openness to the discomfort of being different from someone you care about. In the next chapter we will deepen our relational skills so that we can tackle these exact kinds of challenges. Sex is just one example of a kind of activity we must discuss and negotiate with people in our lives. In relationship anarchy, everything is on the table. Let's dig in.

CHAPTER 5

Practicing, Fucking Up, and Embracing the Messiness

We've discussed many aspects of relationship anarchy so far. The hard bits, the delicious parts, the social and emotional challenges, and the historical context. But how do we bring all these pieces together to create something tangible? How do we invite people to show up for us in genuinely impactful ways? I can imagine how nice it would be to fall asleep in a friend's arms when I'm feeling lonely, but how do I go about asking for that, negotiating the boundaries, and defining our relationship moving forward? What tools do we have for the messy, chaotic, and scary parts of this relationship journey? Relationship anarchy can be full of cuddles, laughter, and community care, but there is hard and complex work through every relational journey.

EXPERIENCING REJECTION

When we start to explore our authentic desires, we are faced with a choice: Do I share these desires, knowing they may not be reciprocated, or do I keep them to myself and protect myself from potential rejection? There is no clear right or wrong way to navigate our hearts. Sometimes we crave something that we know isn't going to be possible, and it might feel better to process that grief alone or within a safe community. Other times, we are faced with a frightening reality: The only way to find out is to ask.

I recently experienced this first hand. I value honesty in my relationships. If I notice feeling romantic or sexual desire for a friend it often feels important to name that. There are certainly exceptions to this: If I don't have capacity to pursue romance or sexual connection it doesn't feel as pressing to name unless it's become a very noticeable part of our dynamic. In this particular case, I found myself right on the cusp of friendship and romantic desire. Every time I hung out with this particular friend I noticed my desire to touch them, flirt with them, and get close to them. None of these things are oppositional to a healthy friendship, but I wanted to make sure that my friend and I were on the same page. And, I kept noticing myself imagining us on a date together. I needed to get clarity, so I asked them.

I started by sending this friend a text asking if they'd be willing to receive a voice memo with a share about my feelings. I did this for two reasons. One, I wanted to get their consent to share something vulnerable over voice memo. I don't want to assume that other people always have space for me or my feelings. Two, I know that getting a heads up about something intense can help prepare a friend to receive that information. I wanted to offer us both containment and holding.

My friend said yes, go ahead and share. I spent several hours thinking about what I was going to say. Do I keep it brief or explain my detailed emotions? Do I ask them on a date or ask them what they want for us? It took me a while to settle on something that felt authentic without being too vulnerable. Here is what I settled on.

> "Hey friend. Take your time to respond to this. I wanted to check in with you because I've been noticing that I've been feeling some more crush-y and romantic feelings for you. I'm super down to continue to be friends, but I wanted to ask if you'd like to go on a date and see how that feels. Let me know when you can."

And then I had the urge to throw my phone into the street.

The visceral and overwhelming sensations in my body were very informative! This was a lot for me. Despite trying very hard to be authentic and honest, my fear of rejection is so intense that it's terrifying to imagine being with myself while I experience rejection. There was also the possibility that my friend wanted to go on a date, which was terrifying in its own way. Did I actually want to be vulnerable, or did I just want to stay in the fantasy of being vulnerable?

I share this story to illustrate that as someone who has been practicing relationship anarchy and non-monogamy for almost ten years, I still regularly feel like a fourteen-year-old asking their crush to the school dance for the first time. I've gotten really skilled at communicating, *and* my internal world is often very fragile and sensitive. Relationships are so scary! I often say to one of my partners, "I'm devoted to you, not our relationship." I love people based on who they are, not the relationship structure they can offer. However, that doesn't mean I don't get sad when my desires don't link up with others' desires.

My friend took about twenty-four hours to respond to the voice message I sent. In that time, I went through a wide variety of feelings. From panic to regret to euphoria to calm to neutrality to fear to excitement—oh my goodness it was a ride! At one point I called one of my partners to get some emotional support. It was so regulating to talk to someone who loves me. They reminded me of four essential aspects of being authentic, especially if rejection is possible.

1. Without relinquishing responsibility for my impact on others, I can acknowledge that the way other people respond to me is more about them than me.
2. Being authentic and honest with others is a gift to myself and to them.
3. There is nothing shameful in feeling desire.
4. My feelings of desire are more about me than about the person or things I feel desire for.

Let's break down these nuggets of wisdom, because wow, they are so helpful!

First, my love reminded me that however my friend responds, it's not a reflection of my value or worth. If someone doesn't find me attractive it doesn't make me unattractive. If someone doesn't crave to kiss me, it doesn't make me unkissable. If someone can't meet me in the emotional place I currently reside in, it doesn't mean I'm in an unlovable place.

Second, when we choose to be authentic, we invite authenticity in others. This is a gift. We can model and normalize honesty, actively shifting the dominant culture of our society which is rooted in concealment, deceit, and theft. To name our truth is to sit squarely in the power of our existence. To say, *this is what it is for me* is to honor the unique *and* shared emotions of the human experience.

Third, it is okay to want things. There is a way to desire that is not violent towards others. Unfortunately, in a white supremacist culture, to desire something is considered the same as giving yourself permission to steal it. In white supremacist culture we are taught there are no boundaries on what you can take, if you want it enough. We are encouraged to consume, hoard, and crave what isn't ours. This is not the only way to desire. We can also desire something while rooted in the knowledge that we may not receive it. We can long for someone, yearn for them, without acting upon these feelings with violence and coercion.

Fourth, whatever the reason I desire someone, my feelings of desire come from within me and are primarily about me. I can think of countless desirable things about the people I love: their personalities, energies, laughter, sense of humor, the feel of their bodies, the way they hug. I desire these things because of my experience of what makes things nice to be around. This is also true of those around me. What people like about me is a reflection of what they have experienced thus far in life that has brought safety, pleasure, and joy to their bodies. It is a joy to activate pleasure in someone else, but it is not a reflection of my inherent self.

When my friend responded, they let me know they were grateful to receive my request, but they wanted to pursue a long-term loving friendship with me. It was interesting to hold the rejection of romantic connection with the invitation of intimate friendship. I'm grateful that the work I've done to deconstruct relational hierarchies allowed me to receive this invitation of friendship as deeply meaningful.

Later that day I spoke to a partner on the phone about this scary moment of asking my friend out. They were so gentle and kind with me. I didn't feel judged or ridiculed for needing emotional support. When we affirm that there's nothing shameful about feeling desire for connection, it's a lot easier to hold the intensity of disappointment. At one point I said, "I'm realizing I really want to feel wanted and like someone wants to go on a date with me."

"I want to go on a date with you," they responded.

"You do?" I asked, feeling extremely squishy.

"Yes! I would love to. You would be so fun to go on a date with."

In this moment my partner affirmed that desiring a cute date with a cutie is not a weird or bad thing to crave. They reminded me that my desire exists in my body, not in the person I asked out. I am the one who wants to go on a date; I am the one who wants sweetness and romance; I am the one who craves complex messy friendship and lover and partner connections all wrapped into one. I don't know what other people want unless I ask them, but whatever it is they do want doesn't invalidate what I want.

In life we do and say things that may spark or activate another person, but the specific reaction to what we do is out of our control. There is no predetermined response to any behavior. While this perspective can absolutely be used to avoid accountability or perpetuate harm (i.e. I can't make you feel bad so anything I do to you is not my responsibility), it can also be a really freeing way to think about our relationships with others.

I find this perspective to be especially helpful when navigating rejection. So often we are projecting our ideal version of someone onto them without their consent. When a person doesn't match up with our imagined version of them, it can feel as if our love is being rejected, when really our projection is being rejected. This is why communicating with the people around us is so beneficial. When we communicate with others and ask them about their experience, we can update our perception of who they are.

I had a perception of my friend that they were a potential romantic partner. I experienced in my body desire for them because they're delightful and they emulate a lot of the qualities that I find attractive. However, I didn't know exactly what their experience of our dynamic was until I asked them. Which is why I asked! When they told me that our connection feels like friendship, and they want to prioritize our friendship moving forward, I was offered an opportunity to update my experience of my desire.

When this delightful human was giving me big long hugs my brain was going "Wow this is great we should do more touching." Now that I know that for them those big long hugs were big long *friend* hugs, I can update my experience of them and our hugs. We can still have lovely hugs (if we both want to), but it's my responsibility to honor the agreement of our relationship by respecting our hugs as friend hugs.

If there comes a time when I don't feel I can engage with their hugs without inserting a different narrative, then we'll need to have another conversation. Sometimes we have to set boundaries with people in order to protect their boundaries. It wouldn't be fair to my friend to keep them in a romantic place in my mind when that's not where they want to be. If I'm not able to update my experience of them to friendship, then they deserve to know that, and act accordingly. In some situations, this could be fine. I have a friend right now who

I share a mutual romantic interest with, but because of the circumstances of our life we have decided to stay friends and not pursue those feelings. But the feelings and the romantic energy are welcome in our friendship. This works for us now, and it may not work forever. We are both responsible for staying curious about how things feel between us.

Rejection is an invitation. If we accept this invitation, it will lead us into deeper clarity and insight about our feelings and our connections with others. That doesn't mean that rejection doesn't include sadness, fear, and pain. It is so normal to hurt when someone doesn't want the same thing we do. In order to receive rejection with love, we need to grapple with our capacity to be with big and painful feelings like fear.

BEING WITH OUR FEARS

If there's one thing I've learned over and over again, it is that this work is scary as fuck. I regularly feel scared. I feel scared of being honest, scared of asking for what I want, scared of saying something embarrassing or shameful. I feel scared of being rejected, abandoned, and betrayed. I feel scared of intimacy, touch, and falling in love. Being a deeply loving, authentic person is really scary! Sharing what you want from people in your life, rather than following the scripts given to us by society, is terrifying. What if the people I love don't accept me anymore? What if they think I'm weird or broken? What if I push them away? What if they push me away?

I regularly hear my clients ask themselves and their partners, "What is the point of doing this hard work?" If relationships can cause us to feel so much discomfort and pain, why keep doing them? In my Navigating Non-Monogamy workshop

I start by asking participants to answer the question "Why non-monogamy?" I've found that when we feel connected to our own unique reasons for doing something, it's easier to bear the suffering that comes with that experience.

So let's explore this question of why. Why do you want to explore relationship anarchy? I invite you to reflect on this question, journal about it, and discuss with people in your life. Your answers may be very obvious to you or you may be unsure of your why. Whatever comes up for you is okay. When we ask ourselves *why*, we open ourselves to the fear of the unknown. We may not know why, and we may experience our why morph over the course of our life. All of that is okay.

In my interviews for this book, many people reported that exploring relationship anarchy offered them a deeper understanding of themselves. When I asked interviewees what they might want someone new to relationship anarchy to know, it was common for folks to say, "This is not easy, but it's rewarding" or "Don't forget to remind people it's hard but worth it!" I appreciated the passion with which my interviewees expressed this nuance. I often got the sense they were speaking to a part of themselves who felt, or perhaps once felt, unmoored and overwhelmed. The people who had found a relationship orientation that is working for them wanted me to remind everyone who is still searching that there is hope.

We can learn to sit in the discomfort of our feelings. We can befriend our fears and anxieties. We can build our relational skills for communication and connection. We can heal intergenerational and lifelong wounds. The roadmap to achieving these things is being created in this very moment as you read and reflect and breathe. I hope to offer some road signs along your path. As you read about the many tools, insights, and skills we've collected, I hope you take what is helpful and leave what is not for you. At the end of the day there is only you and your body and your willingness to ask the question, what is it like to be me?

As we explore, pay attention to your somatic experience of fear. What does it feel like to be afraid? Does your pulse quicken? Do you get sweaty or hot? Do you feel shutdown or numb? Can you breathe when you're scared? Can you give or receive care? What is possible when your body is afraid?

In order to be with fear, we have to practice being with fear. In order to build our capacity to be with fear, we can slowly and carefully expose our body to scary experiences within a container of relative safety. This is a process of stretching our window of tolerance, the space that exists between flight, fight, freeze, and fawn responses. This is the space of relative regulation in which we can stay present with our somatic sensation, responses, and emotions. That doesn't mean that this window of tolerance feels easeful or pleasurable all the time. Learning to be with fear often involves riding the line between regulation and dysregulation, sometimes finding a sweet spot in which we feel supported to take risks, and other times slipping into dysregulated responses because a situation was more challenging or scary than we thought it would be. *Becoming dysregulated is not bad*; it's a sign that our bodies need care and compassion. We can offer this care through self-soothing and/or co-regulation, depending on who and what is available at the time.

Self-soothing is the process of comforting and supporting ourselves when we're experiencing an intense emotion or sensation in our body. Your body naturally gives you signals that you're experiencing something intense; this could look like an increased heart rate, more rapid breathing, or panicky thoughts, and/or numbness, feeling like you're in a dream, and being unaware of your physical body. These are just a couple of things you might experience. We can respond to these signals with attention and care, the way we would respond to a child or animal who was in distress. If I came across a small scared being I would want to create a space in which they were safe enough to feel their feelings and move through the embodied responses they were having at their own pace. We can do this same containment for ourselves with self-soothing skills. I'm going to share a list of self-soothing tools you can use, and then I invite you to write your own or highlight any of mine that you might want to try. Which of these activities might feel supportive when you are distressed?

Self-soothing:

- Cuddle a pet.
- Cuddle a blanket or stuffed animal.
- Take care of another plant/animal/person.
- Cry.
- Journal.
- Do something creative.
- Give a voice to your inner child (write a letter).
- If a partner is on a date, give yourself treats before/ during/after a date.
- Make a plan with a partner to receive a treat or gift from them in the future.
- Make your own self-soothing list.
- Make your own dysregulation care plan.
- Develop intimacy in platonic relationships (touch, vulnerability, care).
- Clean your room/make a nice space to be in.
- (With consent) share shadow thoughts/feelings with partner/friend.

- Practice a sacred/spiritual ritual.
- Do a spell.
- Move your body.
- Sit with the feeling, noticing all the sensations.
- Ask for help, call a friend.
- Write a letter to past or future self.
- Write an encouraging letter to yourself, imagining you're a close friend trying to hype yourself up.
- Make good food or beverage.
- Take cbd or natural remedies.
- Take a bath.
- Listen to music.
- Dance freely/interpretative dance your feelings.
- Take hot selfies.
- Read a book.
- Take a class on something you're curious about.
- Spend time in nature.
- Sit with the feelings some more.
- Masturbate.
- Go on a date (alone or with someone).
- Watch a favorite movie.
- Read a favorite book.
- Meditate.
- Learn a new skill.
- Make art/draw/paint.
- Plant a plant/care for a plant.
- Go to the park.
- Look at flowers.
- Do yoga/stretch.
- Make a fort.
- Film yourself/someone else/something.
- Make an altar.

- Climb a tree.
- Lie on the floor.
- Order take out.
- Give or receive impact play.
- Do a kink scene/bdsm.
- Go on a walk.

You may have noticed that some of these suggestions involve other people, because self-soothing and co-regulation are intertwined processes. Co-regulation is the process of regulating our bodies with the aid of another being. This can range from soothing touch, a validating conversation, or taking deep breaths together to simply sitting in the same room, or thinking about someone you care about to remember they exist.

Self-soothing and co-regulation are such valuable relational tools because they offer a balm to the challenges of being in a human body. However, some things can't be soothed. It's important to hold these skills in balance with the reality that sometimes our bodies cannot immediately process or hold ongoing and/or intentional harm. When our bodies continue to feel immense dysregulation without relief, it can be a sign that there is something in the relationship that is unsustainable. This brings us to an exploration of challenges versus dealbreakers.

CHALLENGES VERSUS DEALBREAKERS

Relationship anarchy supports autonomy, independence, interdependence, and self-exploration. In relationship anarchy we don't embark into our exploration without boundaries, agreements, and clear communication. Humans are messy, and there are inevitably going to be mistakes, missteps, and misunderstandings. Sometimes these pitfalls can be transformative opportunities. We can delve deeper into intimacy and understanding. Other times, they are markers of incompatibility or abusive tendencies. So how do we identify the difference between discomfort that is necessary for growth versus cues from our body that we are truly unsafe? Let's explore this question!

I'm going to share some different scenarios with you. Read through each story once, just taking in the information. Then read the story again. As you read, place yourself in the story. Which character do you identify most with? How might you react to such a situation?

1. Sabina and Clare have been dating for five years. They feel a lot of trust and love in their relationship. They don't live together and that feels good for both of them. They love hiking together and going out for drinks with friends. Four years ago, Sabina kissed one of their close mutual friends, Elle, while Sabina and Elle were hanging out alone. It was a passionate kiss, but Sabina felt guilty the whole time. After the kiss, Sabina told Elle she didn't want to kiss again because she wanted to be with only Clare. She never told Clare about the kiss because she didn't want to do anything that could lead to a breakup. Elle moved away shortly after, so in Sabina's mind it didn't seem necessary to bring up. Recently Elle moved back and asked to meet with Clare and Sabina together.

2. Miguel and Leo have been non-monogamous together for two years. The first couple of times Miguel went on a date, Leo felt so upset that he couldn't sleep or eat. Miguel is getting ready to go on a date, and he notices

that he can't stop worrying about Leo. He tells Leo he is considering canceling his date. Leo gives Miguel a big hug and tells him that it's up to Miguel, but he doesn't need to save him from feeling bad.

3. Peri, Eloise, and Dequan live together in a platonic triad. Whenever Peri is upset they yell at Eloise and Dequan. They know it's hurtful to their partners to yell, but they get so flooded they don't know how to stop. They always apologize after they yell, but Eloise and Dequan still feel like they have to walk on eggshells to avoid their anger. Eloise and Dequan love Peri, but they don't know if it's worth staying with them. They often wonder if Peri will ever be able to speak to them gently when they're upset.

Notice your physical and emotional responses. How does it feel in your body when you think about each situation? What kinds of images, sounds, sensations, energies, or movements are evoked as you read? What questions do you have about these situations? What information would you need in order to make sense of the situation?

Now read each passage again and try putting yourself in another character's shoes. What changes in this role? Can you see both sides of the situation or is it difficult to empathize?

In the example of Sabina, Clare, and Elle I am reminded of how important it is to let our partners consent to the relationship they are in. By keeping the truth about her kiss with Elle a secret, Sabina is taking away Clare's right to consent to the relationship they are in. It makes sense that Sabina doesn't want to hurt Clare, or herself, by risking a breakup, but at what cost? In order to consent to a relationship we need information about what is happening in it. Clare, and

Sabina, deserve to choose each other because they want to choose each other, not because they are operating on false pretenses.

The second example poses a difficult non-monogamous conundrum: Should Miguel stay home with Leo and support his partner or trust his partner can withstand hard feelings and choose to go on his date? There isn't one right answer to this question. As long as Miguel is clear on his own boundaries, he can decide how he wants to interact with Leo's feelings. By reminding Miguel that he doesn't need to save him from feeling bad, Leo is affirming that Miguel is not directly harming Leo. Miguel gets to choose: Is it possible to tolerate Leo's feelings of distress when he's on a date, or does Miguel need to stay home from his date to stay regulated? Miguel might want to pay attention to stories he's telling himself about how much discomfort is okay for Leo to feel. It's not Miguel's job to rescue Leo, but it's also okay to care about how someone you love is doing.

We all have different relationships with anger. Some people are comfortable with raised voices, but most people experience persistent yelling as extremely damaging. This can absolutely be considered verbal abuse. If Eloise and Dequan feel like they can't exist around Peri without fear of being yelled at, it's time to set some boundaries. Eloise and Dequan might want to individually consider how long they are willing to tolerate Peri's reactivity before they leave the relationship. They might each also think about how they will interact with Peri when Peri yells, including leaving the house or closing a bedroom door. Because the three of them live together, it could be time to discuss a new housing arrangement.

Each one of these examples gives us a window into how complex relationships can be. Something that is challenging to one person might be a dealbreaker to another. Depending on our relationship to trauma, neurodivergence, community, and material resources we might be inclined to put more or less energy into a relationship.

In all these situations, safety is paramount. If you feel unsafe around someone to the extent that you worry about your emotional or physical well-being, it's time to evaluate the situation. Be sure to check the section at the end of this book for resources on navigating abusive situations.

In non-abusive relationships, there is still often a question of: How much of this can I tolerate? That is a question that only you can answer, and whatever answer you come up with is okay. We are not required to give anyone love, connection, time, or energy. It is always okay to leave a relationship, no matter how deep or meaningful it has been up until then. Further, in relationship anarchy "leaving" a relationship does not necessarily mean cutting off all ties or connection with that person. It is possible to love someone from afar. It is possible to rejoice in someone's humanity without sharing an intimate partnership or connection with them.

If you do decide to continue a relationship with someone, you can also consider how the relationship structure might change in order to be more supportive to everyone involved. In order to make these changes, sometimes we need to lean into conflict and get clarity on what is possible between people.

NAVIGATING CONFLICT

Conflict is a hugely broad term to describe so many different experiences. Conflict is the experience of being at odds with someone or something else. We experience conflict when we want pasta for dinner and our pal wants soup. We experience conflict when a well-intentioned friend says something that hurts. We experience conflict when we rub against our deepest, most core differences. We experience conflict when we continue to live in a world that does not prioritize or value our existence.

Some conflicts are quickly resolved with simple compromises. When we can't decide what to have for dinner we can get creative or compromise. Maybe we make two dishes for dinner, pasta and soup, or we make a soup with pasta in it! This may seem trivial, but being able to stay in conflict long enough to find a solution that works well enough for everyone can be truly strenuous. It takes practice to stay creative in the face of conflict. When our brains go into fight/flight/freeze/fawn, we lose access to creativity and executive function. It can be helpful to practice staying open to compromise when the stakes are low, so we can build our resilience when things get more charged.

But how do we behave when something truly heart wrenching happens and we want to repair it with someone even though we're scared of further hurt? The people we love often have the greatest capacity to hurt us emotionally. There is no clear script for navigating these ruptures. Part of developing our relational skills is developing our attunement to our inner experience. When we have access to information about how we feel, the sensations of our body, and the emotions and stories of our inner world, we can make informed decisions about how we want to navigate conflict with people in our life.

I asked Moss how they navigate communication with their partners when challenges arise.

I have to intellectualize it first and understand it before I let myself feel it (if I even let myself feel it, but that's another talk). But being able to show up for that little part of me that's like, "No bitch, this hurt my feelings and here's why" and coming back to it is important. I kind of do feel like a kid when I do it where I'm like, "Hey bud, do you have some time to talk on this date? I, I wanted to let you know how a thing felt to me last time we hung out because it didn't feel pretty good. I would really benefit from being able to tell you this and not sweep it under the rug because like, you know, I'm working on the way that I show up in conflict." So, a lot of the time it's kind of clunky like that for me right now. I'm learning how to do that more smoothly.

I invite you to pause here and re-read Moss's example of inviting a friend to discuss something that hurt them. How does this example sit with you? Does it feel like something you might say or not at all? Write down a couple example scripts of how you might ask someone to talk about something that hurt your feelings.

The next time you experience a conflict, notice what it is like for you! Pay attention to whether or not you want to retreat, repair, or stay in conflict. You might ask yourself or someone else: How does this conflict feel right now? What do I need in order to make room for empathy and honesty? Does it feel safe enough to be in this conflict?

PROTECTIVE IMPULSES IN CONFLICT

Can you think of a time you chose conflict? Perhaps you're someone who regularly leans into conflict, or maybe you're someone who avoids conflict at all costs. For many of us, there are situations in which our body will let us know it's time to lean into conflict with someone else. We all have a biological mechanism that will let us know it is time to "fight," but our fight response on its own does not always achieve the results we crave.

I am reminded of something Alaina Knox explained to me about working with partners who are navigating conflict. Sometimes with attention and care the conflict can be resolved, and other times, that is your special conflict that you get to keep coming back to over and over. Might as well get familiar with it.

John Gottman developed his practice through helping couples navigate conflict and build long-lasting relationships. Many people believe that long-lasting romantic relationships are the most valuable and fulfilling relationships, so offering tools to help married couples stay together has been extremely lucrative. Gottman studied the markers that lead to long-term satisfaction in romantic relationships. The research began with heterosexual couples but has since expanded to queer relationships. However, it continues to be grounded in white and monogamous frameworks. For that reason, it's imperative we maintain an intentional reflectiveness of how these dynamics may play out differently among different cultural groups. Let these concepts be a starting point and not an ending.

Gottman identified the "four horsemen" of relational communication patterns that were likely to lead to divorce. These four horsemen are criticism, contempt, defensiveness, and stonewalling. Criticism is different from sharing frustration or annoyance; it is an attack on someone's character. A blog post on the Gottman Institute web page written by Ellie Lisitsa (n.d.) offers the difference between a complaint and criticism.

Complaint: "I was scared when you were running late and didn't call me. I thought we had agreed that we would do that for each other."

Criticism: "You never think about how your behavior is affecting other people. I don't believe you are that forgetful, you're just selfish. You never think of others! You never think of me!"

Do you tend towards complaint or criticism? How do you respond when someone shares a complaint versus a criticism? In what situations might you be called to share a complaint or criticism?

The second horseman, contempt, can be understood as a feeling of disgust or complete disregard for another's humanity. Contempt often shows up as being mean, cruel, or completely lacking in empathy for another's experience. A 2015 study found that couples in a relationship with persistent contempt were more likely to experience infectious disease (Hysi 2015).

When have you felt contempt for someone? Do you feel contempt for people you know intimately? Do you feel contempt for people you've never met? How do you act around people you feel contempt for?

Have you ever noticed someone feeling contempt for you? What did it feel like? How did you go about protecting yourself from someone's contempt?

Defensiveness is a common response to feeling attacked or misunderstood. It's a way to protect ourselves from harm by refusing to admit that we have made, or are capable of making, mistakes. Defensiveness, like all of these four horsemen, is a protector. Defensiveness tries to keep us safe from criticism or contempt. Instead of shaming yourself or your partner for feeling defensive, you may want to be curious about why defensiveness is arising. This is true of all the four horsemen. Instead of judging yourself for being critical, ask, "Why do I feel the need to criticize?" Instead of shaming yourself for feeling contempt, ask, "Why can't I connect to my empathy for this person?"

How does defensiveness show up in your life, in yourself or others? What kinds of behaviors or responses help you drop your defenses?

The fourth horseman is stonewalling, which is another way to say shutting down completely. Stonewalling is another protective mechanism that may keep us safe from contempt, criticism, or any other number of unpleasant interactions. Stonewalling protects us by removing our perception of all emotions, positive, negative, and neutral. When stonewalling, we may keep someone else out, but we also stay disconnected from ourselves.

When do you use stonewalling to try to keep yourself safe? Are there times you want to hide from everything, including yourself? Do you ever notice people in your life stonewalling? What might be making them feel unsafe?

These four horsemen are not death sentences for a relationship, nor are they unique to romantic relationships. This framework can help give us cues for when things are becoming tense in a relationship. When this occurs, it is necessary that we address these conflicts, which will undoubtedly bring up intense emotions. The challenge is that we often end up in cycles of criticism, contempt, defensiveness, and stonewalling when we don't have healthy pathways to engage in conflict. When conflict feels insurmountable or terrifying, these protective mechanisms come to our aid.

What is your relationship to conflict? Do you tend to avoid

the situation, hoping it will pass with time, or do you deep dive into what happened, trying to avoid any repetition? Do you believe that conflict is inevitable, or do you seek to avoid it whenever possible? Does conflict bring you closer to the people in your life, or does it cause more rifts?

Many of us find that we avoid conflict because the fear of being alone and the fear of being socially ostracized are often greater than the fear of spending our lives with people who may not see or understand us. What if we didn't have to choose between being alone and feeling celebrated? Humans need to feel like the people around us are delighted by us. There is so much pressure on us to find and keep romantic relationships that many people stay in relationships where they don't feel very appreciated or loved.

Further, in some relationships, people do feel appreciated and loved, but conflict is still terrifying because it feels like a slippery slope to chaos and disconnection. If you associate conflict with danger and/or violence, it will be very scary for your body to engage in conflict. Those of us who live with the impacts of trauma may be familiar with the panic that accompanies someone getting angry or upset, perhaps especially when the person is yourself.

So how do we navigate conflict with care, even when our bodies are terrified?

STAYING CURIOUS

So often we make split second decisions about partners, responses, communication, and conflict when we really need more information. Start getting curious before you get certain. Pay attention to the information people give you from the very beginning. Maya Angelou said, "When people show you who they are, believe them the first time." Believe people by paying attention to who they are and being curious about who they'll become.

Consider these questions as you build your connections.

1. Ask: Is consent prioritized?
2. Notice: Is there accountability for successes and mistakes?
3. Consider: Is there space for rupture and repair?

As you develop your knowledge of a new person, their ins and outs, preferences, and quirks, there is a simple question we can ask that can reveal so much about someone's inner world: *What do you want to hear right now?* The goal of this question isn't to coerce or convince a partner into saying something that isn't truthful. This question invites a curiosity into how someone is experiencing the relational moment. Let me give you a concrete example with a dialogue between two friends, Alan and Kell.

Alan: I'm feeling super angry and frustrated that you bailed on me again. I thought I meant more to you.

Kell: I hear you're angry and frustrated. I'm wondering what you want to hear right now.

Alan: I want to hear you say that you won't ever do this again.

Kell: That makes sense. I get that this was really hurtful. I don't want to promise something I can't keep, but I do understand that if I do this again there will be consequences.

Alan: I just wish there was a way I could be promised safety in this relationship.

Kell: That makes sense. Are you feeling scared to trust me? I wonder if we can slow things down and rebuild at a pace that feels okay to you.

Alan: I want to trust you again. I don't want to feel this fear because I really love you. But, if I'm being honest with myself, trust has been broken and it will take time to repair.

Kell: Yeah, I know it will. I want to take that time. I don't expect you to trust me again yet.

Let's pause and look at this interaction! We hear Alan telling Kell that they want to feel safe and that they want to know that Kell won't hurt them again. That is such a deeply understandable and human thing to desire. Is it possible? Not really. No one can promise us that they will never hurt us again, and it's unwise to try. I see Alan expressing that they feel very unsafe and that they don't trust Kell in the way they used to.

Kell affirms and validates Alan's feelings. They are able to sit in the discomfort of not being trusted by Alan instead of trying to fix or push away these feelings. From here, Kell might inquire about how Alan wants to be supported at that moment. For example, "I hear that you don't feel safe and that you don't want this to happen again. Do you want to talk more about these feelings, or do you want to discuss a practical plan to support us both in the future?" This is an example of our next communication tool. Kell is asking Alan: Do you want emotional support or problem solving? So many relationship and communication challenges can be resolved with this question. Depending on your unique experience of relationships and relational trauma, you may find that it's easier to lean into emotions when someone is upset or to lean into problem solving. When we are connecting with someone, it's important to avoid assumptions about how they want to be supported. Let's dive into an example!

I have a very problem-solvey mom. My mom is great at research, data collection, and creating practical solutions for problems. She is the number one person I go to when I need help navigating bureaucracy, editing a book, or trying to plan a trip on public transportation. I love these qualities in my mom, and I find them to be incredibly loving. *And*, there have been many times in my life in which I really needed her just to sit with me attentively while I cried, affirm my feelings, or help me explore why I feel a certain way. I noticed from a young age that this space-holding work often made her uncomfortable and even shut down. As she shut down, my feelings became more intense. I was trying desperately to get the response I needed: something like "Oh my gosh this hurts so much for you. I see you're in so much pain. I see that this is not going to be solved right now."

Instead, I often got the message that my feelings were problems that needed to be solved. Over time, I stopped going to my mom with my raw emotion. But, I never stopped wanting her to hold space for my feelings.

As an adult we've been able to have more transparent conversations about this dynamic. When I am able to clearly express that I don't want problem solving from her, she listens. She began developing patience and compassion in herself for big messy emotions that felt scary to her. I know my mom's problem-solving impulse comes partly from wanting to make me feel better, to take away the negative or challenging emotions, and partly from her own discomfort with intense emotions. To develop a more supportive relationship, she had to acknowledge the reality that trying to "fix" my feelings made them harder for me. She also had to stretch her own capacity for discomfort, pain, sadness, anger, and hurt.

My intense feelings spoke to parts of her that had been exiled for years. She never got the chance to safely feel her emotions, so it was scary to let me do it. Our relationship is in flux, like all things. We haven't arrived at a perfectly symbiotic dynamic in which we both always feel loved and supported, but we have both gained much more insight into our emotional landscapes. When I do speak to my mom these days, she has so much more capacity for my messy feelings than she used to. I'm learning to be okay with the fact that she may never have as much capacity as I need now or as I needed as a child.

Let's come back for a moment to Alan and Kell. If Kell says, "Do you want problem solving or emotional support right now?" or some variation of this that Alan understands, and Alan responds, "I want emotional support," then the two of them can pivot to validation, listening, and noticing the sensations coming up. If Alan responds, "I want problem solving" then the pair can start diving into tools and solutions. But what if Alan responds, "I don't know, I have no idea." Where do we go from here?

This is a dynamic I see come up a lot in the relationship work I do with couples. One person states a specific request or suggestion, and the other responds with some variation of a panicked "I don't know!" It's helpful to remember that many of us have never been directly asked what we need or how we feel. It can be intensely vulnerable to be asked what you need, especially if you're not sure yourself. There is a very understandable desire in many of us to have our people understand us on such a deep level that they can assess and deliver what we need directly to our doors. Maybe we even want them to come inside and unbox the package and set it up for us.

It makes sense, because this is exactly what parents must do for children. Babies need us to identify and meet needs for them as quickly as possible. If we fail to do so, babies will let us know by crying and screaming. Crying and screaming are an extremely effective way to get someone's attention, but it's a difficult way to communicate with nuance and clarity what you need. One of my favorite human things is when parents can tell with striking accuracy what kind of cry their baby is crying. The sounds of an "I'm hungry" cry and an "I'm sleepy" cry are different! Still, it's markedly easier when children arrive at a point where they can say "I am hungry," or "I am sleepy." And even then, as we get older, our emotions become more complicated. It's not common for a child to be able to articulate their needs in such a nuanced way as, "I am hungry, but I am also sad which, is why I want this particular food and none other will do. Also, I'm sleepy because we had a big day and I had my feelings hurt at the playground which was really hard for me, so I'm feeling extra exhausted. Which is also why I'm so hungry right now."

Many of us have parts of ourselves that still operate in this childlike headspace. There is nothing wrong with that, just as there is nothing wrong with babies needing their parents and kids saying "I'm hungry" when they mean "I'm also sad." What I have found is that the real question is: Whose responsibility do you think it is to meet your needs? Does this responsibility change depending on the environment you're in? Do you feel responsible for meeting other people's needs? When and how often?

I'm genuinely curious to hear your responses to this question! It is one that I ponder regularly. How do we balance the responsibility we all carry to meet our own needs with the reality that as humans we need other humans to meet our needs? It is our responsibility to get our needs met, but we cannot meet our needs on our own. We need to delegate in order to receive care and love. We cannot expect our people to read our minds, but we can expect them to become aware of our emotional landscape. We can expect people to do things to support us, regularly, and with consistency. We can expect people to try to ease our suffering. However, we need to clarify what these things are and acknowledge the limitations of support. Once we get consent and agreement, we can trust others to show up for us! I am very specifically saying we *can* do this. Not that we must or that we should. Not that we will or that we have to. We can do these things, with practice, intention, and support.

Now, let's explore some prompts that might help you determine what you want and need from relationships.

- How much housework/chores would I like a housemate/partner to do? How much would I like to do?
- How do I want to feel when I'm hanging out with [insert relationship here]? What sort of vibe do I want to create?
- How do I like to be cared for when I'm sick?
- Do I prefer to have someone ask me questions about how I feel, or give me space so I can share in my own time?
- What is non-negotiable in a relationship? Can I think of any situations in which these would change?

As you reflect on these questions you might notice your resistance and/or excitement in sharing your insights. Let's explore how and why we communicate with people, and the ways communication can be muddy or clear.

COMMUNICATION STYLES

What is your experience of communicating vulnerable or sensitive information to people around you? Have you ever explored the different communication styles you might utilize?

The Princeton University website[1] offers an excellent and concise description of four different communication styles that I'm eager to explore with you. I'll outline them below so we can discuss! Please keep in mind that these four styles are certainly not the only ways to communicate, nor do they encompass all the nuances of human communication dynamics. However, it can be really helpful to have a framework through which to explore our experience of communication. Use this framework to deepen your exploration, not to draw black-and-white conclusions.

Passive communication is defined as using evasive or unclear language and behavior to avoid direct conflict or tension. Passive communication can be extremely beneficial when navigating unsafe situations—it often places the nexus of choice on the other person, which can be helpful when someone is unpredictable. However, passive communication can also lead to confusion and uncertainty.

Aggressive communication often involves ignoring or diminishing others' needs and wants in favor of your own. It can include yelling, making derogatory or mean comments, and prioritizing your own story over others.

Passive aggressive communication can seem similar to passive communication on the surface, but is actually aggressive just under the surface. Passive aggressive communication often includes sarcasm, eye-rolling or judgmental looks, and

---

1   umatter.princeton.edu

undertones of anger or discontent even when someone says everything is "fine." Passive aggressive communication can be confusing for everyone involved because it's often the result of two or more different internal impulses fighting to be heard. People who often use passive aggressive communication don't feel comfortable being outright aggressive, nor do they feel comfortable attempting a more direct mode of communication.

Assertive communication (or direct communication) is a communication style that respects others' words, space, and feelings at the same time as your own. Assertive communication expresses clearly the information you have about your own experience, even if this information is limited. Sometimes assertive communication can be misinterpreted as aggressive communication, especially when being received by a more passive communicator.

These communication styles usually merge and combine when we interact with others.

Human communication is incredibly nuanced and includes things like context and mutual agreement. In relationship anarchy, we are faced with the delight and the challenge of navigating a lot of unique relationships with care. Due to this, it's common for folks to experience challenges with communication. Even if you are the most effective, direct communicator out there you will likely run into people you really care about who don't always communicate very directly. This is a factor of being in a relationship with others. More important than trying to force ourselves into shapes that don't feel good, we can notice the shapes, patterns, and habits we fall into when communicating with others and course correct when needed.

Let's look at some different communication examples and get to know your communication landscape more intimately!

We can use the example of asking a friend on a date to explore these different approaches.

Using passive communication: Would you ever go on a date with someone like me?

Using aggressive communication: I'm gonna keep asking you to go on a date with me until you say yes.

Using passive aggressive communication: Nobody ever wants to go on a date with me.

Using direct communication:

1. I've really enjoyed getting to know you. Would you want to go on a date with me?
2. I think you're so brilliant and fun. Can I take you out?
3. I know we're friends now, but I'd be interested in exploring something more romantic between us. How do you feel about that?
4. I'd love to hang out with you again. I really like you.
5. I'm definitely interested in you. I have so much fun with you.
6. I'm really excited to get to know you better. I'd love to learn more about your romantic and sexual desires.
7. I know we just met, but I feel really drawn to you. Any chance you'd want to get to know each other better?
8. I'm noticing I feel really sexually attracted to you. How are things between us feeling for you?

What kind of communication style feels most familiar to you? Do you find that you lean toward a certain style? Do you dabble in all the styles depending on your state of mind? I invite you to pay attention to your words the next time you communicate with someone. How can you be more clear? How can you be more honest? And if it doesn't feel possible to be more clear and honest, why is that?

As we practice communication, we will certainly find ourselves in moments of miscommunication. Even when we use direct language, meaning can be lost between people. Sometimes our tone or body language communicates much louder than our words, which can be confusing on all sides. In these moments, we can only do our best to acknowledge the uncertainty of interacting with other humans. While sometimes misunderstandings cannot be repaired, there is so much that can be transformed when we meet each other with curiosity, authenticity, and honesty.

Being authentic and honest is a gift to ourselves and others. Many of us are trained from a young age to suppress our feelings. When we move through the world dampening down our desires, we deny ourselves so many experiences. Instead of naming confusion, hurt, or misunderstanding we might silence ourselves in order to keep the peace. Staying small can protect from grief, rejection, and sadness. But what if we didn't think of hard feelings as a bad thing to feel? Is it painful? Yes. Is it big and intense? Absolutely. Also, suffering can be a window into our desire. When I am disappointed, I realize with depth how much I was craving something. That craving, that yearning, is part of my life force. And when someone I desire so deeply is lost or inaccessible, it deserves a grieving process. We deserve to feel hurt! We deserve to feel the depth of grief that comes with desire. And we deserve to be held through these feelings.

If this seems really abstract and kind of confusing to

you—yes! It is. It feels like a complex thing to hold in my brain and my body. Have you ever had a conversation with someone in your life about these kinds of dynamics? If not, what would it be like for you to open a channel of communication around desire, suffering, and emotions? If yes, how do you relate to these concepts so far? What do they inspire in you?

Part of what I'm naming is the process of negotiating how we feel and perceive each other with the specific things we do together. As a sex educator, I've taught many classes on very sexy topics in situations where being aroused openly was not appropriate. I've often given the guidance to my students of noticing arousal in their bodies without pointing it at anyone.[2] I see this as being a practice of taking responsibility for our feelings without requiring other people to hold them.

In relationships, what if we could collaborate with the people around us instead of projecting our desires and expecting them to satisfy us? In the example I shared earlier about asking a friend on a date and receiving the response that they only wanted to be friends, I definitely felt sad and disappointed. I also felt relief, because now I can actually engage with this friend in a way that is feeling good for them. From this point, there is a huge amount of potential for me and my friend. All I know right now is that this person wants to be my friend. But what exactly does that mean to both of us? And how do we go about creating the friendship that we want? The next step here is to ask my friend what they would like us to do together. I mean this in small and big ways. It might be helpful for me and my friend to look at the relationship anarchy smorgasbord and talk through what we are craving.

When I interviewed Atira, I asked them how they determine

---

2   I was first introduced to this by Roz Dischiavio at ISEE.

the kind of relationship they'd like to have with people in their life. She explained the process of figuring this out with her current partners.

Basically I remember asking both of them, "How would you like me to refer to you? Like a partner?" For one partner, I used boo for like a long time and then we had a relationship check-in and I was like, "Is it cool if I refer to you as a partner?" Also...for my current romantic partnerships, I've done a "define the relationship" type worksheet... And I literally have spent hours with both my partners going through this list and be like, all right, financial, emotional investment...going through each section. For some people, I can imagine that could be like a lot, a lot. But I find relationships and human behavior fascinating and probably one of my special interests and hyper focuses. So I'm like, let's talk about it. I think for me, even for dating, it's a green flag when the partner is very into it because I had a previous partner who when I asked, "Do you want to do this work?" they responded, "Oh, this feels like a lot. I don't know." At the time I was like, oh okay, but it was probably also indicative of, maybe it's not a good fit. But for one of my current partners, I remember mentioning how I did this with my other partner and he was just like, "That sounds amazing. I would love to do a 'define the relationship' meeting workshop with you."

It's a really good fit for me and at least for myself, it also forced me to interrogate what are the things that I actually want in this relationship. Like, what is important to me and what is maybe not that important? So it's good for myself to just have clarity on what are the things that I want in my life potentially with this person. And I can do generally but also specifically, and it's really good to be that specific because I think I remember someone said when it comes to specificity, it just allows for accountability,[3] you just like, out here. Yeah. So that's the thing, I was just like being in a relationship with one another. Part of that is being helpful to one another. So, what are the ways we want to be accountable to one another? I'm like, this is a very good way to get very specific about what that looks like.

There are all kinds of resources and visuals on the internet that can help us explore these concepts with people we care for. Try googling "Relationship Anarchy menu" or "Relationship Anarchy worksheets" to open that can of worms! These resources help us clarify the kinds of logistical things we want to do with our people. I asked Alex Alberto (they/them), a queer genderfluid person, how they navigate prioritizing friendships. They shared a non-monogamous bread-and-butter tool: Google Calendar! They put regular check-ins for friends and partners on their Google Calendar so that all their relationships are tended to with regularity and intentionality. We can also use a calendar to help conceptualize the way we are dividing our time with our people. As a visual person, I find it helpful to look at my calendar each week and see how much time I've allotted to my different activities. My ADHD brain has trouble keeping track of things and remembering when I last saw someone, but my calendar helps me keep track of what I'm up to.

What kinds of structures or containers might you need in order to facilitate conversations? Do you have a regular

---

3   In Atira's words: "I got this idea from Priscila Garcia-Jacquier and her (now defunct) social media presence involving anti-racism work around deconstructing Latinidad! They're no longer on social media, but here's her site: https://www.priscilagarciajacquier.com/"

check-in with partners/friends/loves? What might help you feel supported to bring grievances or feelings to the table?

HOLDING MISTAKES

One thing you will find if you start asking people about relationship anarchy, is that there are some people who manipulate relationship anarchy concepts to control and abuse others. For those of us who are navigating relationships ethically, it feels important to communicate that while relationship anarchy is not easy, it's also not inherently harmful. However, that doesn't mean that harm doesn't happen. Part of building a more ethical relational world involves taking responsibility for the harm we cause and centering the healing of those we harm. Relationships are activating, and when activated, we are at risk for behaving hurtfully or without awareness. How do we hold space for the wounds that get activated, without recklessly re-traumatizing ourselves? How do we center others when harmed?

In all relationships, we make mistakes. In relationship anarchy many of us find that there are more opportunities for miscommunications, hurt feelings, fear, insecurities, and activation of attachment wounds. It's inevitable that you and the people you choose to relate to will make mistakes and it will suck.

There are, of course, different levels of fucking up. Some of us will navigate painful missteps and well-intentioned miscommunications. Others will grapple with betrayal, deceit, and abuse. I take an abolitionist approach to relationships: I do not believe that punitive actions are necessary in order to protect survivors of harm and abuse. I also believe that humans who harm others are deserving of transformative healing, therapeutic interventions, and basic kindness. This co-exists with the establishment of boundaries, consequences, and accountability processes.

There is no easy way to address the reality that you've hurt another human. It is my firm belief that in order to grapple with the pain of making a mistake (or mistakes), we must access the suffering we've experienced when harmed. If it's difficult to access the grief of your own hurt, it may be because there are one or many parts in you that are working tirelessly to protect you from this pain. We may have parts that believe feeling the depth of this hurt will ostracize us further, become so overwhelming we cannot function, or even kill us.

This framework of "protective parts" comes from the theory of Internal Family Systems (IFS), a therapeutic approach that was first developed by Richard Schwartz in the 1980s. It has been explored and utilized by many therapists over the past 40 years. It has inspired my relationship anarchy approach for addressing conflict and rupture when you are the one who has caused harm. This method is also effective when harm has been caused on both or all sides. This approach to harm is not intended to keep relationships alive or people together. It is not meant to be used to disregard abuse or invalidate the impact of anyone's actions.

The structure of this method consists of five questions we can ask ourselves to guide our parts and our core self to a deeper understanding of the harm we've caused to others without resulting in further ostracization or forced solitary confinement. In IFS we take the approach that "everyone is at their core a Self containing many crucial leadership qualities such as perspective, confidence, compassion, and acceptance" (Schwartz n.d.). Our parts are separate from a core self; they may be young, old, angry, helpful, frustrated, organized, chaotic, meek, non-human, or any other conglomeration of images, thoughts, feelings, sounds, sensations, and features our human bodies can configure.

When you find out you've harmed someone else, ask these five questions. Take your time with each question, using words, images, sounds, movements, sculpture, food, or another form of self-expression to consider the answers that arise in you.

Who inside me is trying to protect me?

How do I feel toward myself?

When have I been hurt? What did it feel like and how is it present now?

What do I need in order to be accountable for my actions?

What does the person I hurt need?

When we harm someone else, we must find space in our bodies for the feelings that arise because we caused harm. These feelings might include fear, shame, anxiety, frustration, anger, resentment, and so many others. What kinds of sensations exist for when you realize you've made a mistake? Many humans feel fear when they harm someone else, because humans are hardwired to seek acceptance and support from other humans. When we do something hurtful, we become aware of the potential that we could be ostracized or rejected. Have you ever heard the saying, "Bravery is not the lack of fear but the conviction to do what you need to do in spite of fear"? I would alter that saying to this: Bravery is the conviction to try something even while you're afraid. Taking responsibility for your impact on someone else is brave. I invite you to try. And if it doesn't work for you, I invite you to try again in six months, or a year, or twenty years from now. There is no roadmap for this work. You get to go at your own pace. You get to stumble, make mistakes, and keep trying.

When we make mistakes, we must reckon with the right of other humans to decide how they want to interact with us. This could look like someone wanting to change or shift the relationship we have. As terrifying as this can be, trying to force someone to stay often makes them leave quicker and go further away. There is a radical power in affirming someone's choice to respond to our actions however they need to. Relationship anarchy invites us to constantly reckon with our desire to control others and lovingly release this impulse. Our relationships will change; we get to decide if we will embrace and welcome change, or try to punish ourselves and others for needing to change.

CHANGING RELATIONSHIPS

Everything on this earth exists in cycles of beginning and ending. A flower grows, buds, blooms, and wilts. Its petals return to the soil and decompose, providing nutrients to the bugs and plants that grow from it again. The same atoms reform and regrow, starting over again, budding and blooming again. We are all in constant cycles of change, and these cycles overlap onto each other. We can be falling in love and breaking up at the same time, seeing each other more intimately than we have before in the moments of death and grief.

Our relationships are endless cycles, ebbing and flowing with the tides and seasons.

As a 19-year-old first-year college student living in Portland, Oregon, I met someone who would come to be my first romantic love and one of my most formative relationships. Zee and I met at a Talking Heads dance party hosted at my college. They were going to school across the Willamette River at Lewis and Clark. I went to Reed College in the heart of southeast Portland. I noticed them across the tiny dorm room where we gathered to pregame before going to the "ball." They had dark curly hair and a gentle, sweet, sexy manner. I felt immediately drawn to their quiet energy. I beelined over to them and asked what they were drinking. They gave me a swig of their whiskey, and we locked eyes. I love thinking about this moment. I had no idea then how many times I would gaze into this person's eyes. How many tears I would shed, of joy and grief, because of our connection. I had no idea that we would traverse the boundaries of love in so many iterations and become soulmates.

Zee and I dated romantically for about a year before we opened our relationship. Both of us are queer and we felt interested in exploring other dynamics we didn't get from each other. Still, I was hesitant to explore non-monogamy. Romantic relationships felt scary and dangerous to me. What would stop someone from lying, betraying me, or abandoning me? Why would I want to bring more chaos and uncertainty into my life when we could be safely monogamous? I felt intellectually interested in the idea of non-monogamy *and* I felt terrified. Zee made it clear they wanted to be non-monogamous long term, but they were flexible about when that came to fruition. I started reading non-monogamous texts like *The Ethical Slut* by Janet W. Hardy and Dossie Easton (2017) and *More Than Two* by Eve Rickert (2014). The relationships described in these books felt absurdly idyllic. I could imagine falling in love with two people at the same time myself (I already had), but the idea of knowing my partner was having sex with, kissing, holding, and sleeping next to someone else made me feel sick to my stomach. In all these visions, when my partner was with someone else, I was nothing to them. My brain couldn't wrap itself around the idea that I could still be loved, present in my partner's heart, and important in the relationship even when I wasn't there, even when they were with someone else.

Zee has a special kind of relaxed and grounded energy that helped me build safety with them. They were patient, letting me arrive at non-monogamy in my own time, from my own perspective. It wasn't until I went to study abroad in France that I realized non-monogamy could potentially be amazing. Out of my comfort zone and surrounded by hot people who wanted to kiss me, I felt curious. I experienced a budding desire to kiss one of my classmates, and I was surprised to find I wasn't any less interested in Zee. When I shared my desire to kiss this French cutie with Zee they were incredibly supportive. I felt unsettled by how supportive they were, knowing in myself that if the tables were turned I would be spiraling. But they spoke to me like I was their best friend: "Of course all these hotties want to kiss you, beeb. You're a hottie. I'm stoked for you, you're having that experience." I remember a distinct shift in this moment, being held and accepted by Zee, being celebrated in my desires. It reminded me of my safest place: friendship. A place where you can tell someone all about your hot sexual encounters, crushes, and potential partners. A place where I could show up in my slutty queer self without fear of abandonment or shame.

Why couldn't it be like that in my romantic relationship too? Zee started to show me it could.

Early on in our relationship, Zee and I discussed *how* we wanted our relationship to end. It might sound cryptic or depressing, but it felt so incredibly loving. We often said, I can't wait to be your best friend once we're done dating. It became a kind of guiding tenet of our relationship, an intention that we revisited often. One day driving towards home I remember turning to Zee and saying, "I'm not ready to be your best friend yet, but when I am, you're going to be such a good best friend to me." They laughed. "What about you? Are you gonna be a good friend to me?" they asked. "Probably," I joked, "we'll have to see!"

I can't pinpoint exactly how Zee and I have managed to traverse romance to friendship with such gentleness. Perhaps it's our inherent compatibility, our neurodivergence, or our commitment to creating radically ethical communities of care. Perhaps we're just lucky; we managed not to hurt each other too much and held on to love even when it hurt. Our relationship transitions have not been without grief, conflict, and hurt. At times we've needed weeks or months of space from each other. We've had long, hard conversations and tearful goodbyes as things shifted. I know some part of me will always grieve our romantic relationship. And, I can say with confidence that my relationship with Zee has been one of the most fulfilling and safe relationships I've ever experienced. Currently, we don't live in the same place, but we make regular plans to visit each other. We don't have a sexual relationship, but we hug, cuddle, and kiss each other on the cheek. We talk on the phone every couple of days, and we text (or share memes) almost every day. Our relationship is committed, consistent, and joyful. We know each other's partners, and we share many friends.

We recently discussed using our reproductive capacities to make a baby someday.

An amazing aspect of relationship anarchy is that we get to create relationships that feel authentic, intimate, and special in their own ways. I once made friends with one of the smartest, funniest, most charming people I'd ever met. I found them to be simply delightful. We became fast friends, naturally leaning into intimacy like sleepovers, sharing our heartaches, and leaning on each other for emotional support. This friend, Ollie, was in a monogamous relationship at the time with another lovely human who I also enjoyed hanging out with. After we had been friends for about a year, Ollie's partner, who had already graduated school, moved away, and the two began a long-distance relationship. During this time my friends began discussing non-monogamy. The first time Ollie told me about this, I felt a flutter in my stomach. I was happy being Ollie's friend, but I was also aware that I felt more complicated feelings towards Ollie than I had expressed. I didn't want to compromise our relationship, my friend's relationship, or my friendship with Ollie's partner. As Ollie and their partner began discussing their changing relationship, I became aware that I was feeling deeply invested in Ollie and their partner trying to be non-monogamous. I wanted Ollie to be non-monogamous so that I could ask them out.

What I noticed is that I was feeling more invested in getting what I wanted than I was invested in my friend experiencing a life that was right for them. Once I realized this, I was faced with the decision of either accepting my initial reaction or trying to shift my viewpoint. I decided that I wanted to practice loving my friend no matter what they could offer me. When I sat with it I realized that my love did transcend romantic or platonic labels—I wanted this person in my life, however it felt best to us. While it was hard to let go of the expectations of our dynamic changing to something romantic, it didn't actually stop us from exploring this dynamic. Ollie and their partner decided they did want to explore non-monogamy, and I was able to tell Ollie about my feelings towards them. I expressed that it felt weird to hope they would be non-monogamous so that we might have a chance to date, but that I wouldn't hold anything against them no matter what they decided. They shared that they never felt pressured by me, and that they trusted in their own ability to make the right choice for them. We continued to embark on a complex and multifaceted relationship, one that contained erotic exchange, romance, friendly laughter, emotional support, studying and work support, sleepovers, group friendships that included other people we love, and periods of varying intimacy depending on what was going on in our lives.

In order to tell someone we want to change our dynamic, we have to be honest with them. It's important to recognize the motivations we have for sharing our desires and identify how available we feel to someone's rejection. A common phrase in sex positive and sex education spaces is "If you can't give a no, you can't give a yes." If there is not space for someone to say no to something, is saying yes even an option? I find this framework to be helpful when assessing if we truly have space for someone else's experience. It doesn't mean that disappointment, hurt, or anger aren't allowed when someone says "No." It does mean that we own these feelings as our responsibility, and we don't expect others to fix us or soothe us past their capacities.

CHAPTER 6

Explore the Manifesto

When Andie Nordgren wrote the relationship anarchy manifesto, she helped continue a conversation about how we want to deconstruct current norms *and* build our relationships simultaneously. The manifesto is straightforward and approachably concise. Now that you've journeyed through the great expansive world of relationship anarchy, let's read these words together and discuss how this manifesto can help us build and continue our conversations about ethical and loving relationships! After each section of the manifesto I will guide you with some reflective questions and interactive tools to deepen your thinking. As you read, consider what kind of manifesto, poem, dance, speech, book, or essay you might create to share your approach to relationships.

Love is abundant, and every relationship is unique

Relationship anarchy questions the idea that love is a limited resource that can only be real if restricted to a couple. You have capacity to love more than one person, and one relationship and the love felt for that person do not diminish love felt for another. Don't rank and compare people and relationships — cherish the individual and your connection to them. One person in your life does not need to be named primary for the relationship to be real. Each relationship is independent, and a relationship between autonomous individuals.

Do you feel like you have the capacity to love multiple people? How many friends could you have? How many partners? How many family members?

Take a couple minutes to respond to this prompt in conversation or in writing:

Think about two or three people in your life who you love. How would you describe the way you feel towards each of them? In what ways does it feel similar or different to love these people? Are there ways you feel uniquely seen or understood by these people?

Love and respect instead of entitlement

Deciding to not base a relationship on a foundation of entitlement is about respecting others' independence and self-determination. Your feelings for a person or your history together does not make you entitled to command and control a partner to comply with what is considered normal to do in a relationship. Explore how you can engage without stepping over boundaries and personal beliefs. Rather than looking for compromises in every situation, let loved ones choose paths that keep their integrity intact, without letting this mean a crisis for the relationship. Staying away from entitlement and demands is the only way to be sure that you are in a relationship that is truly mutual. Love is not more "real" when people compromise for each other because it's part of what's expected.

What do you notice as you read this? What does it feel like to imagine not compromising and instead letting loved ones do what they feel is right even if it's hard?

Here's a prompt to deepen your thinking: Journal or discuss!

How can we identify the difference between overriding our needs and boundaries and respecting a partner's choices and autonomy? When is it appropriate to ask for a compromise, and when is it appropriate to sit with our feelings?

Find your core set of relationship values

How do you wish to be treated by others? What are your basic boundaries and expectations on all relationships? What kind of people would you like to spend your life with, and how would you like your relationships to work? Find your core set of values and use it for all relationships. Don't make special rules and exceptions as a way to show people you love them "for real".

Do you find that you immediately know the answer to some of the questions posed, or does it feel challenging to come up with a response? Make a list of core values you have in your life. This might include honesty, respect, integrity, humor, resilience, compassion, empathy, or many other things! Once you make a list, go back and try to define each of these terms. Can you think of any situations in which you would be willing to compromise or change your values for a relationship?

Heterosexism is rampant and out there, but don't let fear lead you

Remember that there is a very powerful normative system in play that dictates what real love is, and how people should live. Many will question you and the validity of your relationships when you don't follow these norms. Work with the people you love to find escapes and tricks to counter the worst of the problematic norms. Find positive counter spells and don't let fear drive your relationships.

When I first read this section I thought, what is a counter spell and how do I find it! What is your response to reading this? Do you find that you're already impacted by systems of oppression like heterosexism or is this a new thing to you?

I invite you to notice your capacity for being counter-cultural. Here are some questions that can help guide this exploration. Do you feel comfortable speaking up when you hear someone say something harmful? Do you find yourself choosing forms of self-expression (hair, clothes, body adornment, etc.) that are considered "typical" or more non-normative? Do you make these adornment choices because you want to or because you feel like you have to? Do you exist in a body that is often perceived as different than how you feel inside? How much fatigue or frustration do you experience from being othered?

Build for the lovely unexpected

Being free to be spontaneous—to express oneself without fear of punishments or a sense of burdened "shoulds"—is what gives life to relationships based on relationship anarchy. Organize based on a wish to meet and explore each other— not on duties and demands and disappointment when they are not met.

How do you make sense of chaos and spontaneity in this world? Do you like to have everything in order before you embark on something new, or do you jump in and figure things out as you go along? What is your capacity for messiness? What scares you about the unknown? How much uncertainty can you sit with?

Fake it 'til you make it

Sometimes it can feel like you need to be some complete super human to handle all the norm breaking involved in choosing relationships that don't map to the norm. A great trick is the "fake it 'til you make it" strategy—when you are feeling strong and inspired, think about how you would like to see yourself act. Transform that into some simple guidelines, and stick to them when things are rough. Talk to and seek support from others who challenge norms, and never reproach yourself when the norm pressure gets you into behaviour you didn't wish for.

How do you feel about the fake it 'til you make it strategy? Have you ever felt forced to behave in a way that was inauthentic to you? How did that impact you? How important is it to you that you get things right the first time you try them? What is it like to feel the gap between who you are now and what you might become? Who do you want to be?

Trust is better

Choosing to assume that your partner does not wish you harm leads you down a much more positive path than a distrustful approach where you need to be constantly validated by the other person to trust that they are there with you in the relationship. Sometimes people have so much going on inside themselves that there's just no energy left to reach out and care for others. Create the kind of relationship where withdrawing is both supported and quickly forgiven, and give people lots of chances to talk, explain, see you, and be responsible in the relationship. Remember your core values and to take care of yourself though!

What happens in your body when a partner doesn't have space for you? Did you feel trust as a younger person that your caretakers would come back? Do you feel trust in yourself to be with feelings that arise when you're alone?

Change through communication

For most human activities, there is some form of norm in place for how it is supposed to work. If you want to deviate from this pattern, you need to communicate—otherwise things tend to end up just following the norm, as others behave according to it. Communication and joint actions for change is the only way to break away. Radical relationships must have conversation and communication at the heart—not as a state of emergency only brought out to solve "problems". Communicate in a context of trust. We are so used to people never really saying what they think and feel—that we have to read between the lines and extrapolate to find what they really mean. But such interpretations can only build on previous experiences—usually based on the norms you want to escape. Ask each other about stuff, and be explicit!

What is your relationship to open communication? Do you know what you feel? Do you know how to communicate these feelings? Do you find it hard to tell people what you want and need? Do you ever feel frustrated by others for not saying what they mean?

Customize your commitments

Life would not have much structure or meaning without joining together with other people to achieve things—constructing a life together, raising children, owning a house or growing together through thick and thin. Such endeavors usually need lots of trust and commitment between people to work. Relationship anarchy is not about never committing to anything—it's about designing your own commitments with the people around you, and freeing them from norms dictating that certain types of commitments are a requirement for love to be real, or that some commitments like raising children or moving in together have to be driven by certain kinds of feelings. Start from scratch and be explicit about what kind of commitments you want to make with other people!

What kinds of things do you hope to experience in this lifetime? What are your life goals? What is possible in the context of your job, family, environment, and home? What kinds of commitments do you want to experience with others? Who do you want in your life, and what do you want to do with them?

FINAL THOUGHTS

The relationship anarchy manifesto is a great example of a starting place to deepen our thinking about relationships that work for us. There is nothing in this book that is fixed, certain, or universal. I hope you can use these ideas to get closer to what you and your community need. As you embark on your relational journeys, I hope you can continue to pay attention to what brings you closer to your authentic, radical truth.

As you affirm your ability to be in relationships as your full self, I wonder what will happen? I already see the cracks forming in the oppressive society we live in, but it takes real people creating real relationships in order to grow like stubborn trees up through the cracks and towards the sky. I hope you leave this book with a deeper awareness of your connection to others. Your impact on others matters.

As we near the end of this book, I find myself thinking of my friend Alex, who died in 2020 at 26 years old. He was one of the most loving, open-hearted people I've ever known. In college it seemed that everyone wanted to be his best friend, and it often seemed there wasn't enough time in the day to hang out with him. He was always on his way to a party, or a concert, or a day on the river, or holed up in his room reading *Mrs Dalloway* again. I sometimes felt annoyed that he didn't have more time for me, but I also felt grateful I got to know him at all. There was one day, after he died so suddenly, that I went to sit on my back porch and grieve. I was rocking in a hammock, looking out at the beautiful Oakland trees feeling the bright, warm sunshine on my face. I felt an immense gratitude in that moment for every second Alex had been loved, whether I was present or not. In his short life (but really, how long are any of our lives?) I am so glad he soaked up every last bit of love that he could. I am so glad that I didn't let my desire to love him prohibit him from being loved by anyone else. I wanted him to have all the joy, all the play, all the laughter possible. In that moment the finite quality of this life was so tangible; the love we give people is not fleeting or meaningless, it is the substance of our precious lifetimes. I will still feel jealous, scared, uncertain, and angry in my relationships, but I understand now the stakes of my love. When I grieve my loves I will do so knowing that I did my very best to make this world loving for them. And that includes all of you, reading this. I hope you'll join me in making this world worthy of your precious lives.

Resources

FURTHER READING

Ace: What Asexuality Reveals About Desire, Society, and the Meaning of Sex by Angela Chen

All About Love: New Visions by bell hooks

Bisexual Men Exist: A Handbook for Bisexual, Pansexual and M-Spec Men by Vaneet Mehta

Healing Sex: A Mind-Body Approach to Healing Sexual Trauma by Staci Haines

Hopeless Aromantic: An Affirmative Guide to Aromanticism by Samantha Rendle

More Than Words: The Science of Deepening Love and Connection in Any Relationship by John Howard

The Developing Mind: How Relationships and the Brain Interact to Shape Who We Are by Dan Siegel

The Jealousy Workbook: Exercises and Insights for Managing Open Relationships by Kathy Labriola

This Is Supposed to Be Fun: How to Find the Joy in Hooking Up, Settling Down, and Everything in Between by Myisha Battle

Trans Sex: A Guide for Adults by Kelvin Sparks

Trans Sex: Clinical Approaches to Trans Sexualities and Erotic Embodiments by Lucie Fielding

Transition: Understanding and Managing by Personal Change by Barrie Hopson, John D. Adams and John Hayes

INTERVIEWEES TO CONNECT WITH

Che Che Luna (they/them), @che.che.luna, https://checheluna.com/

Cleopatra Tatabele (they/them), @afrobrujx, www.cleopatratatabele.com

Sydney Rae Chin (they/them), @sexysoupdumplings, sexysoupdumplings.com

Yael Rosenstock (she/her/ella), @yaelthesexgeek, www.sexpositiveyou.com

SOCIAL MEDIA

@adventuresofpolycat

@bear.n.fifi

@bygabriellesmith

@chillpolyamory

@drlaurenfogelmersy

@drlizpowell

@femislay

@gottmaninstitute

@hijadetumadrela

@irene.morning

@lavitaloca34

@polyamorousblackgirl

@polyamorouswhileasian

@polyrolemodels

@poly_inclusion

@poly.lovers

@remodeledlove

@shrimpteeth

@somaticwitch

@the.holistic.psychologist

PODCASTS

Adventurous Polyamory

All My Relations

Amory

Bad in Bed

Double Teamed

Enemies2Lovers

Glamorous and Polyamorous

Just Be Poly

Loving without Boundaries

Life on the Swingset

Making Polyamory Work

Modern Love

Monogamish

Multi Monogamous Podcast

Multiamory: Rethinking Modern Relationships

Non-Monogamy Help

Normalizing Non-Monogamy

Nope! We're Not Monogamous

Playing with Fire

Poly Pocket Podcast

Polyamory in Black

Queer and Poly

Ready for Polyamory

Remodeled Love

The Kitchen Sink, ENM and Kink Podcast

The Modern Loving Family

The Poly (Pod)Cast

The Polyjamorous Podcast

The Neurodivergent Polyamorist

Throuple Talk

AND MORE...

Love Is Respect, loveisrespect.org

National Domestic Violence Hotline, www.thehotline.org

RAINN: National Sexual Assault Hotline, https://hotline.rainn.org/online

The Anarchist Library, theanarchistlibrary.org

FOR YOUTH AND TEENS

Relationship check-up, https://nysyouth.net/relationships/great/checkup.cfm

Scarleteen, scarleteen.com

Bibliography

Addison, S.M. and Coolhart, D. (2015) "Expanding the therapy paradigm with queer couples: A relational intersectional lens." *Family Process 54*, 3, 435–453.

Akbulut, N. and Razum, O. (2022) "Why Othering should be considered in research on health inequalities: Theoretical perspectives and research needs." *SSM—Population Health 5*, 20, 101286.

Aune, K.S. and Wong, N.C.H. (2002) "Antecedents and consequences of adult play in romantic relationships." *Personal Relationships 9*, 279–286.

Baldwin, J. and Peck, R. (2017) *I Am Not Your Negro*. London: Penguin Books.

Baxter, L.A. (1992) "Forms and functions of intimate play in personal relationships." *Human Communications Research 18*, 336–363.

Betcher, R.W. (1977) "Intimate play and marital adaptation: Regression in the presence of another." Doctoral dissertation, Boston University, 1977. *Dissertation Abstracts International 38*, 1871.

Black, B. (2012) "Anarchy 101." In *Defacing the Currency: Selected Writings, 1992–2012*. Berkeley, CA: LBC Books.

Black, B. (n.d.) "Anarchy 101." The Anarchist Library. https://theanarchistlibrary.org/library/bob-black-anarchy-101

Blair, C. and Raver, C.C. (2016) "Poverty, stress, and brain development: New directions for prevention and intervention." *Academic Pediatrics 16*, 3, S30–S36.

Blue, A. (2022) *Social Commentary and Killing the Cop Inside Your Head with MoMa PS5*. To Be. https://tobemagazine.com.au/social-commentary-with-moma-ps5/

Bowlby, J. (1958) "The nature of the child's tie to his mother." *The International Journal of Psychoanalysis 39*, 350–373.

Bowlby, J. (1969) *Attachment*. Attachment and Loss, Volume I. London: Hogarth.

Bowlby, J. (1988) *A Secure Base: Parent-Child Attachment and Healthy Human Development*. New York: Basic Books.

Braff, E. and Schwarz, R. (2004) "The power of play in relationships manual." Unpublished manuscript.

Bretherton, I. (1992) "The origins of attachment theory: John Bowlby and Mary Ainsworth." *Developmental Psychology 28*, 5, 759–775. doi.org/10.1037/0012-1649.28.5.759

Brower, N. (n.d.) "Have Fun! The Importance of Play in Couple Relationships." https://extension.usu.edu/relationships/research/the-importance-of-play-in-couple-relationships#:~:text=Purpose%20of%20Play&text=Play%20can%20also%20promote%20spontaneity,Lauer%20%26%20Lauer%2C%202002

brown, a.m. (2017) *Emergent Strategy: Shaping Change, Changing Worlds*. Chico, CA: AK Press.

brown, a.m. (2019) *Pleasure Activism: The Politics of Feeling Good*. Chico, CA: AK Press.

Charles, J.M. (1983) "Adult play." Paper presented at the National Convention of the American Alliance for Health, Physical Education, Recreation and Dance, Minneapolis, MN.

Colarusso, C.A. (1993) "Play in adulthood: A developmental consideration." *Psychoanalytic Study of the Child 48*, 225–245.

Coontz, S. (2005) *Marriage, a History: From Obedience to Intimacy, Or How Love Conquered Marriage*. New York: Viking Penguin.

Coontz, S. (2016) "The Radical Idea of Marrying for Love." *Sun Magazine*. www.thesunmagazine.org/articles/28111-the-radical-idea-of-marrying-for-love

Crenshaw, K. (2017) *On Intersectionality: Essential Writings*. New York: The New Press.

Dana, D. (2021) *Anchored: How to Befriend Your Nervous System Using Polyvagal Theory*. Louisville, CO: Sounds True Inc.

Erping, X., Jing, J., Ze, H. and Jijia, Z. (2022) "The relationship between children and their maternal uncles: A unique parenting mode in Mosuo culture." *Frontiers in Psychology 13*. https://doi.org/10.3389/fpsyg.2022.873137

Fern, J. (2020) *Polysecure: Attachment, Trauma, and Consensual Nonmonogamy*, 1st edn. Portland, OR: Thorntree Press.

Gahran, A. (2012) "Riding the relationship escalator (or not)": Solo Poly. [Blog post]. https://solopoly.net/2012/11/29/riding-the-relationship-escalator-or-not/

Hardy, J.W. and Easton, D. (2017) *The Ethical Slut: A Practical Guide to Polyamory, Open Relationships and Other Freedoms in Sex and Love*, 3rd edn. New York: Ten Speed Press.

Hazan, C. and Shaver, P. (1987) "Romantic love conceptualized as an attachment process." *Journal of Personality and Social Psychology 52*, 3, 511–524.

Hemphill, P. (2021) "A reminder. Boundaries are the distance at which I can love you and me simultaneously." Instagram post. https://www.instagram.com/prentishemphill/p/CNSzFO1A21C/

hooks, bell (2014) "Are you still a slave? Liberating the Black female body." Eugene Lang College. The New School. www.youtube.com/watch?v=rJk0hNROvzs

Hysi, G. (2015) "Conflict resolution styles and health outcomes in married couples: Systematic literature review." Conference paper proceedings. Research and Education "Challenges towards the future" ICRAE 2015. www.researchgate.net/publication/304246577_CONFLICT_RESOLUTION_STYLES_AND_HEALTH_OUTCOMES_IN_MARRIED_COUPLES_A_SYSTEMATIC_LITERATURE_REVIEW

Johnson, D. (ed.) (2018) *Diverse Bodies, Diverse Practices: Toward an Inclusive Somatics*. Berkeley, CA: North Atlantic Books.

Johnson, S. (2008) *Hold Me Tight: Seven Conversations for a Lifetime of Love*, 1st edn. New York: Little, Brown, and Company.

Jones, K. and Okun, T. (2001) *Dismantling Racism: A Workbook for Social Change Groups*. ChangeWork. https://resourcegeneration.org/wp-content/uploads/2018/01/2016-dRworks-workbook.pdf

Kopecky, G. (1996) "Make time for play." *American Health 15*, 4, 65–67.

Kyros, K.F. (2011) "Using marriage to protect white supremacy and heterosexual privilege: A historical analysis of marriage law in the United States". Masters Thesis, Smith College, Northampton, MA. https://scholarworks.smith.edu/theses/539

Lang, S. (2016) "Native American men-women, lesbians, two-spirits: Contemporary and historical perspectives." *Journal of Lesbian Studies 20*, 3–4, 299–323. https://doi.org/10.1080/10894160.2016.1148966

Lardoux, S. and Van de Walle, É. (2003) "Polygamie et fécondité en milieu rural sénégalais." *Population 58*, 807–836. doi.org/10.3917/popu.306.0807

Lauer, J.C. and Lauer, R.H. (2002) *The Play Solution: How to Put the Fun and Excitement Back into Your Relationship*. Chicago, IL: Contemporary Books.

LaVon Rice, A. (2022) "The art of Black, queer, neurodivergent survival." [Blog post]. www.wecreatespace.co/post/the-art-of-black-queer-neurodivergent-survival

Levine, A. and Heller, R. (2011) *Attached: The New Science of Adult Attachment and How It Can Help You Find – and Keep – Love*. New York: Penguin.

Lindgren, J., Matlack, E. and Winston, D. (2021) "339 – The Smorgasbord of Relationships". [Audio podcast episode]. Multiamory: Rethinking Modern Relationships. www.multiamory.com/podcast/339-the-smorgasbord-of-relationships

Linser, R., Lee-Rinstad, N. and Vold, T. (2008) "The Magic Circle – Game design principles and online role-play simulations" (PDF). Ed-Media. www.academia.edu/29026057/The_Magic_Circle_Game_design_principles_and_online_role_play_simulations

Lisitsa, E. (n.d.) "The Four Horsemen: Criticism, contempt, defensiveness, and stonewalling." [Blog post]. www.gottman.com/blog/the-four-horsemen-recognizing-criticism-contempt-defensiveness-and-stonewalling

Mahoney, E. (2022) "Millions of disabled Americans could lose federal benefits if they get married." NPR. www.npr.org/2022/02/13/1080464176/disabled-americans-cant-marry-able-bodied-partners-without-losing-federal-benefi

Markman, H.J., Stanley, S.M., Blumberg, S.L., Jenkins, N.H. and Whiteley, C. (2004) *12 Hours to a Great Marriage: A Step-by-Step Guide for Making Love Last*. San Francisco, CA: Jossey-Bass.

Masterclass (2023) "Relationship anarchy explained: What is relationship anarchy?" MasterClass. www.masterclass.com/articles/relationship-anarchy

Mattsson, T. (2013) "Intersectionality as a useful tool." *Affilia 29*, 1. doi.org/10.1177/0886109913510659

Menakem, R. (2017) *My Grandmother's Hands: Racialized Trauma and the Pathway to Mending Our Hearts and Bodies*. Las Vegas, NV: Central Recovery Press.

Michaels, M. and Johnson, P. (2015) *Designer Relationships: A Guide to Happy Monogamy, Positive Polyamory, and Optimistic Open Relationships*. Jersey City, NJ: Cleis Press.

Murray, M. (2019) "Marriage as a tool of white supremacy." [Audio podcast episode]. At Liberty Podcast. www.aclu.org/podcast/marriage-tool-white-supremacy-ep71

Oyĕwùmí, O. (1997) *The Invention of Women: Making an African Sense of Western Gender Discourses*. Minneapolis, MN: University of Minnesota Press.

Parrott, L. and Parrott, L. (2006) *Your Time-Starved Marriage – Workbook for Men: How to Stay Connected at the Speed of Life*. Grand Rapids, MI: Zondervan.

Pérez-Cortés, J.C. (2020) *Relationship Anarchy: Occupy Intimacy!* 2nd edn. Independently published.

Raffo, S. (2022) *Liberated to the Bone: Histories. Bodies. Futures*. Chico, CA: AK Press.

Rickert, E. (2014) *More Than Two: A Practical Guide to Ethical Polyamory*. Portland, OR: Thorntree Press.

Schwartz, R. (n.d.) "Evolution of the Internal Family Systems Model." IFS Institute. https://ifs-institute.com/resources/articles/evolution-internal-family-systems-model-dr-richard-schwartz-ph-d

Shanae, T. (2018) "The Gap: Social Wounds and Personal Transformation." In D.H. Johnson (ed.) *Diverse Bodies, Diverse Practices: Toward an Inclusive Somatics*. Berkeley, CA: North Atlantic Books.

Smith, K.E. and Pollak, S.D. (2020) "Early life stress and development: Potential mechanisms for adverse outcomes." *Journal of Neurodevelopmental Disorders* 12, 1, 34. doi: 10.1186/s11689-020-09337-y

Tallbear, K. (2016) "Looking for love in too many languages." [Blog post]. www.criticalpolyamorist.com/homeblog/looking-for-love-in-too-many-languagespolyamory-relationship-anarchy-dyke-ethics-significant-otherness-all-my-relations

UMatter (n.d.) "Understanding your communication style." Princeton University. https://umatter.princeton.edu/respect/tools/communication-styles

Vanderbleek, L. (2005) "Couple play as predictor of couple bonding, physical health and emotional health." Unpublished doctoral dissertation, University of Central Florida, 2005.

Van Dernoot Lipsky, L. with Burk, C. (2009) *Trauma Stewardship: An Everyday Guide to Caring for Self While Caring for Others*, 1st edn. San Francisco, CA: Berrett-Koehler Publishers, Inc.

Walker, N. (n.d.) "Neuroqueer: An introduction." Neuroqueer: The Writings of Dr. Nick Walker. https://neuroqueer.com/neuroqueer-an-introduction/

Williams, D. (1999) "Transitions: Managing personal and organisational change." EoS. In *ACDM Newsletter*. www.eoslifework.co.uk/transmgt1.htm

Wilbur, M. and Keene, A. (2019, March 19) "Decolonizing sex." [Audio podcast episode]. All My Relations. www.allmyrelationspodcast.com/post/ep-5-decolonizing-sex

Yurcaba, J. (2021) "'Are you ready to heal?': Nonbinary activist Alok Vaid-Menon deconstructs gender." Nbcnews.com. www.nbcnews.com/nbc-out/out-news/are-ready-heal-nonbinary-activist-alok-vaid-menon-deconstructs-gender-rcna1544

Zevallos, Z. (2013) "Rethinking gender and sexuality: Case study of the Native American 'Two Spirit' people." Other Sociologist. https://othersociologist.com/2013/09/09/two-spirit-people/